Colin S

Only Fools &
White Horses

The epic story of the

first circumnavigation of the UK

by open canoe

Garmoran

First published in 2020 by Garmoran Publishing

 arɯoraɒ
Garmoran Publishing,
Strontian, Scotland

The author asserts the moral right to be identified as the author of this work

ISBN 978-1-913510-00-8

Cover image by Colin Skeath

Book designed, printed and bound in Great Britain by
Biddles Books, Kings Lynn, Norfolk

Only Fools &
White Horses

Contents

Appendixes:

Foreword

Two journeys I made in the early 1990s stood as a pinnacle of achievement in canoe for a quarter of a century. The circumnavigation of Wales with Rob Egelstaff in 1992 covered over 400 miles of coastline including some major tide races. Two years later, with Dave Howie, I sailed a canoe across the Irish Sea - a feat only repeated once in the following 25 years. These trips were, at the time, so outrageous that they forged my reputation in the canoeing world.

I have earned my money as a guide and coach for most of my working life. I have published two editions of a book on canoe technique and appeared in Ray Mears' BBC 2 series where we paddled in the Canadian wilderness.

Colin and Katrina Skeath were just another pair of customers who had booked me for two days of coaching. I took to them both immediately. Their technical skills developed during their time with me, but I would only describe them as moderate canoeists. Colin, however, over a cup of coffee, dropped his big idea on me. He was going to attempt a circumnavigation of the

UK in a canoe with his nephew Davis, who, at that time, had never paddled a canoe.

I tried to keep all expression from my face as I casually probed Colin's knowledge of the sea and queried his resilience for such an endeavour. Bit by bit, critical background information was revealed. Colin and Katrina had recently completed a circumnavigation of Anglesey and had participated in the brutally gruelling Devizes to Westminster race in a racing kayak on a number of occasions. Colin was a proficient climber and had the experience of long multi-day climbs on big walls in Yosemite. He had spent five days of the Nose of El Capitan with another experienced climber. Even more impressive, though, was that he and his nephew Davis had spent nine days on the Muir Wall, each night sleeping on a tiny porta ledge that they hauled up with them. This had been Davis's first venture onto a big wall. I knew then that these guys had one of the essential elements required for a ground-breaking journey - they were mentally tough.

Over the next couple of years, Colin and Davis pushed themselves hard to learn about the environment in which they would be operating. They completed a circumnavigation of Skye and a three-day epic journey covering the River Spey, the Morayshire coast and the Caledonian Canal - both much smaller propositions than the UK circumnavigation but done in difficult conditions. These were critical in building the knowledge they needed.

Even with all their preparation, I still only gave them a 50% chance of success. But as they progressed around the coast, I could see their experience and decision-making grow. Their confidence in their ability and the canoe multiplied many times over. The open water crossings and the conditions in which they were prepared to operate became more outrageous, and their accounts of these fill me with admiration. Gradually, I inched the odds of them succeeding upwards until, after reaching the coast of Wales, I could see nothing stopping them.

So, where does this fit into the greater scheme of things? It was ground-breaking. A phenomenally adventurous small boat voyage which has set a new limit on the possible. However, what makes this such an outstanding book is its honest depiction of the human element. It describes the interaction with everyone from the coastguard and sailors to members of the public who got caught up in this adventure. The relationship between Davis and Colin is laid bare, with all its stresses and triumph. And, although Katrina was not on board the canoe, her land-based support was vital. When everything was at the limit, this was a team that rose to the challenges, both physical and mental. They were exceptional, and I take my hat off to them.

Ray Goodwin MBE (for services to canoeing)

1

Baptism of Fire

Davis had never been in a canoe. This could be considered a slight drawback in that he had agreed to be my partner on one of the longest and most arduous canoe expeditions ever undertaken: the circumnavigation of the UK. So that he could gain some experience, he was to join us in Scotland for a few days of intensive training and warm-up expeditions.

We met at Glasgow Airport and drove to Strontian, a small village on the banks of Loch Sunart. Within an hour of arriving, and with a bit of coaching from Katrina, Davis was paddling a solo open canoe. We were also lucky to have the fine canoeist Greg Spencer and his family join us for a few days to put Davis through his paces. What followed was a whirlwind of intensive training crammed into three days.

I wanted to test our partnership. With eight days to go before Davis was due to leave, we hoped to put his newly acquired skills to the test on a challenging trip. The forecast wasn't promising, but there was a glimmer of an opportunity for a circumnavigation of Skye, the largest island of the Inner Hebrides. This would be a suitably challenging undertaking and a good test of our abilities, but with a weather front heading our way from the Atlantic, we needed to be quick.

Skye has a 400-mile circumference of wild and often remote coast, with promontories extending like fingers from its mountainous interior. Massive cliffs guard long stretches of the coastline with no safe place to land. For Davis, with only three days of canoeing under his belt, and with my limited experience of major expeditions, even contemplating such an undertaking might be considered ludicrous.

Surrounded by equipment and charts of all descriptions, we hurriedly studied tidal flows, printed maps and loaded gear and food for seven days. We planned to be moving continually, using paddles and sails, only stopping to sleep.

The significant tidal hazard we would face was Kyle Rhea, the narrow channel separating Skye from the mainland. Millions of tonnes of water funnel through this gap, generating a fast current against which it is impossible to paddle. Going with the flow means navigating through tidal rapids and whirlpools with the capability of quickly sinking a canoe. To overcome this obstacle, our timing needed to be right – we needed to arrive there when the current was in our favour but not at full strength.

The wind was gusting hard. As we prepared to launch, just west of the Skye Bridge, doubts crept into my mind. A scary sea of white horses could be seen to the west, but, in the sheltered waters near Kyle Rhea, things looked calmer. The wind was due to reduce in strength, so I reckoned that we would be able to get through.

With our battered green 17-foot canoe loaded, we set off, the current taking us down Loch Alsh to the entrance of Kyle Rhea. All was going to plan until the wind was channelled straight into our faces as we entered the narrow passage. One hour in, and we were fighting a battle. Strong gusts of wind against the sail caused the canoe to heel erratically. Waves broke over the sides and water flooded in, almost as fast as we could bail.

Two hours into the expedition, we were well behind schedule and slowly sinking. The realisation hit that we would be at Kyle Rhea when the current was at its most potent. Our bailing buckets were already in overdrive, struggling to keep us afloat as we approached the narrows with naïve optimism.

In front of us was a tide race, and we were on a collision course. The wind against the current was producing steep, uneven waves – an army of white cavalry in line, waiting to rebuff our approach.

Committed to the flow, we found ourselves bouncing, trough to crest, through steep five-foot-high waves. With our buckets bailing hard, we made it through by the skin of our teeth. But it was all becoming too much. We'd had a couple of close calls where only our quick reactions prevented the unstable canoe from overturning. It was only a matter of time before we capsized. The only safe option was to head for shore.

Just three hours into our expedition, we were forced to stop and wait for conditions to improve. Our Skye odyssey wasn't going well.

On the shore, we drank tea and watched the waves gradually ease until, eventually, we were able to continue. To make up lost time, we paddled on, well into the night.

Over the following four days, we canoed through all the daylight hours, regardless of wind or tide. After 14 hours of hard paddling on the fourth day, we capsized. Looking back, this was a gift – an instantly ingrained learning experience.

Davis and I had been relentlessly paddling all day. The sky was dull with a good wind coming from the north east. We had made it around the northernmost tip of Skye to continue south past the soaring vertical columns of Kilt Rock. One more day, and we would be home. The wind drove a swell into the cliffs, resulting in a rebounding clapotis which made for an uncomfortable, nervous time in the canoe.

Searching the coastline for a place to stop for the night, we came close to shore. The swell, although large, appeared harmless enough. The canoe rose and fell as the waves surged under it on their way to the beach, where they broke with a loud boom. As we drew closer to land, the steepness of the swell increased and the water beneath us became shallower. We were parallel to the waves, continuing to scan the shoreline when, in less than a second, I learned that swell and shallow water represents a recipe for disaster.

Instead of passing harmlessly under the boat, the next wave rose into a curling, opaque mass of energy, rising above our heads. We had no chance. In an instant, Davis and I were thrown from the canoe, tumbling into a charging mass of froth. We clung to the boat, trying to reach the shore, but were continually battered and swept off our feet.

After what felt like an age of struggling against the deafening waves with a heavy canoe, we managed to scramble up the boulder beach at the foot of the cliffs and pull the boat onto dry land. We were dishevelled and soaking, and equipment was strewn everywhere between rocks and seaweed, but the only casualties were a slightly bent mast and wet sleeping bags.

As I inspected the damage, I saw Davis talking to a man who had seen our plight from the clifftops. Concerned for our safety, he had rung the coastguard to mobilise a rescue. I couldn't believe that here, in this remote spot, our ordeal had been witnessed. Sheepishly, using my VHF radio, I called the coastguard to report that all was well.

I knew we had been lucky. We were both ok, and the canoe had sustained no significant damage. I had learned to be vigilant in shallow water near rocks – a lesson which was to prove invaluable later.

After a sleepless night, another dull and windy morning saw us back in the canoe, paddling along the Sound of Raasay to finish our five-day circumnavigation of Skye.

The lessons we took from this expedition were to prove essential, and, without this baptism of fire, I doubt if Davis or I would have been prepared enough for our attempt at the UK circumnavigation.

2

Life Defining

I remember it as though it was yesterday – that life-defining moment when I entered the world of adventure.

In 1981, living in the leafy town of Gravesend, beside the Thames estuary, I was a pupil at Thamesview High School. At 14 years old, I was at that awkward age where I thought I knew everything but actually knew nothing. One minute I was confident, the next I was timid. Obsessed with fishing, I used to spend all my spare time in pursuit of carp in the flooded gravel pits and ponds of the Kent Marshes.

Thamesview High was no ordinary school. Through luck or possibly the smart leadership of the head, a group of outstanding teachers collected there. They understood that success in life is not just about how clever you are, and theirs was a holistic approach which valued individual contribution, imagination, courage and initiative over and above performance at exams. This was to my good fortune, as I was more inclined towards sports than academic study.

The principal leader in this mentality was a teacher named Bill Taylor. Mr Taylor, as we knew him, was in his forties.

He had spent three years working for the British Antarctic Survey before becoming a history teacher and head of year at Thamesview High. An imposing, charismatic man with a serious aura, he was both loved and respected by his pupils.

At this time, the school supported an outdoor pursuits group for older pupils. One member of this group was my close friend Philip, who was a year above me. He enthused about the group and suggested that I join. Lured by the promise of adventure, I took his advice as soon as the opportunity arose.

The group was primarily run by Mr Taylor and his fellow teacher and best friend, Malcolm Gilby. Mr Gilby was light-hearted and outgoing – the polar opposite of Mr Taylor – but very experienced in the outdoors. Their personalities complemented each other and, together, they made an inspiring team.

In the outdoor pursuits group, I learned basic skills in how to live in the outdoors, from erecting a tent to camp cooking and map reading. Activities included orienteering and mountain walking, but the main focus was on kayaking.

Once a week, we would travel to a local weir, where a jet of water provided the ideal practice ground for aspiring white-water enthusiasts. Kayaking didn't come naturally to me – I was too stiff and struggled to go with the flow of the boat, guaranteeing capsize and a lot of swimming. I loved the exercise, though, which had the added bonus of involving time outside the classroom.

One Thursday – outdoor pursuits afternoon – it had been dry for a few weeks, and the lack of rain meant that the weir would be low and the paddling mundane. Instead of kayaking, we were introduced to rock climbing.

After an hour in a stifling minibus, we arrived at a small escarpment of rounded sandstone cliffs in a peaceful woodland setting. These were Harrison's Rocks, near Tunbridge Wells in

Kent. Small as they seemed, many people had taken their first steps into serious mountaineering on these crags.

A short walk along a pleasant and wide forestry track took us to the top of the cliff. Ropes, providing safety from above, were arranged around thick tree roots, and we began to climb. My first attempt was a short climb called Bow Window, a 20-foot-high wall with big holds. I remember looking up at the route and thinking, 'this should be easy'. With the rope tied onto my climbing belt, I began to pull myself up the wall, using all my strength to gain height up the small cliff face. But it was desperate – I found the handholds sloped and unhelpful, and my feet were insecure on the sand-covered rock. Halfway up, I was stuck. I was pulling with my arms as hard as I could, but my feet were slipping and ineffective, and my progress stalled. Panting and exhausted, I fell off the rock and was lowered to the ground. I should have been despondent, but, instead, I felt exhilarated. In those few moments, I knew that I wanted to be a climber.

Everything about climbing excited me – I loved the height and exposure, and the feel of the rock. I relished using my strength but knew that I had to learn technique.

I continued to go kayaking with the outdoor pursuits group. We spent adventurous days white-water kayaking at Symonds Yat, and surf and sea kayaking in Pembrokeshire, but my heart was elsewhere. The trips to the Kent Mountain Centre were the ones that fuelled my growing passion for climbing. We would walk up mountains and go scrambling and top-rope climbing.

Mr Gilby gave me my first pair of climbing shoes – an old pair of Pierre Allains (PAs), the grandfather of modern climbing shoes. They were far too big for me, and I had to wear thick socks with them, but they were the best gift I could have received at that time in my life.

To my mother's amazement, I gave up fishing, choosing instead to spend my school holidays climbing. I hitchhiked to the sandstone cliffs of East Sussex and farther afield to Swanage, the Peak District and the Avon Gorge. I had a few climbing friends and sometimes I would meet them, but, if no one was available, I climbed by myself, without ropes.

The next best thing to climbing was reading about climbing. Mountaineering literature was full of gripping and utterly inspiring books such as *The Hard Years* by Joe Brown, a plumber from Manchester who made over 1,000 first ascents. One of my favourite books was *I Choose to Climb* by Chris Bonington, who made the first British ascent of the north face of The Eiger.

An incredible mountaineer who stood out in my mind was Reinhold Messner. In an early account of his climbing, he described how he toughened himself up to handle mountain weather by taking cold showers. In Gravesend, our family home didn't have a shower, so I used to take cold baths instead.

These human stories of life, death, triumph and failure opened up a whole new world to me. They were stories of ordinary people who chose to be climbers and mountaineers, putting themselves in superbly beautiful and dangerous arenas, pushing the boundaries of what was believed to be possible.

~~~

After leaving school, I worked in a variety of manual jobs in London. The pay was poor, and the work was tedious. My escape continued to be the crags and mountains around the UK.

In 1986, I learned that Bill Taylor and two others, Richard Elliott and Mick Wibrew, had completed the first-ever circumnavigation of the UK and Ireland by sea kayak. This impressive feat of endurance is recorded in Bill's superb book, *Commitment and Open Crossings*. I didn't know it at the time, but the seeds had been sown for the first circumnavigation of Britain by open canoe. They would not, however, germinate for another 31 years.

3

A New Obsession

In 1990, by this time married with a young daughter and another on the way, I joined West Yorkshire Police. I couldn't have asked for a more challenging and rewarding career – I loved my work and specialised in neighbourhood policing. Working within the mixed and challenging demographics of West Yorkshire, I felt a strong responsibility to support the people of my community, and did everything possible to tackle offenders, especially bullies who picked on the weak and defenceless. It was incredibly satisfying to see community problems resolved, and enable people to go about their business without worry or hindrance.

During the first few years of my police career, climbing took a back seat in my life. Commitments to my career and my young family meant that I was unable to dedicate much time to any hobby, let alone climbing. I didn't mind, though – my life was filled with things I loved.

But my marriage broke down in 1998, and, following a two-year separation, my wife and I divorced. By this time, I had three beautiful young daughters. Work continued to be a stable and constant platform in my life throughout this time of turmoil. I immersed myself in my job, and I owe a lot to the noble profession of policing, which gave me so much.

The changes in my life opened the door for climbing to once again become important for me. In many ways, I lived a dual existence. On one hand, I was a busy police officer working hard, long hours but, outside work, I was a passionate climber. Most of my time off work, when not with my children, was devoted to the local crags of Yorkshire and Derbyshire when the weather permitted or spent at Leeds Wall, my local indoor climbing centre. For longer breaks, I frequently chose climbing trips to Scotland, Europe, Africa and America.

~~~

I first met Katrina in 2003 in the carpark of Millgarth Police Station in Leeds. I had just dismounted from my BMW motorbike and hung my helmet from the mirror. She climbed off her own motorcycle and approached me, saying, 'You shouldn't leave your helmet like that – it'll get knocked off.'

In fairness, she was right.

At that time, Katrina was working as a police community support officer (PCSO) in Leeds city centre, but she went on to become a detective, working in the extremely challenging environment of child protection.

Katrina was a keen musician with adventure in her heart. I took her to Leeds Wall on our first date. We had so much in common and couldn't get enough of each other's company. Within six months, we had decided to buy a house together in the heart of Scottish climbing country.

We chose a house in the small village of Strontian on the picturesque Ardnamurchan peninsula. The people of Strontian we found to be wonderful, kind folk who genuinely care about each other – we could not have been made to feel more welcome. In Strontian, we were within an hour's drive of some of the country's most spectacular climbing areas.

Some years later, it was here, on the banks of Loch Sunart, that we discovered canoeing.

My climbing had reached a plateau (excuse the pun). At home in the UK, I felt as though I had climbed everything of which I was capable, and was spending much of my time repeating routes. I was training hard to remain at the same standard. I had climbed big walls in America and the Alps, but didn't have the time to take this further, and these areas weren't accessible enough to feed my addiction.

Katrina and I were on holiday in Strontian in July 2010. We planned on climbing, but the weather had other ideas. It was raining, and all of the crags were too wet. We spent our time walking with our two dogs and fishing for mackerel. A wet weather alternative was needed, and we decided to buy a boat to fish from and to explore.

After examining various options, ranging from a small dinghy to a rowing boat, we decided on a canoe as our ideal craft. I was soon to discover all that the canoe had to offer. Almost overnight, my desire to climb slipped away and canoeing became my new obsession.

Our first canoe was a 17-foot-long Old Town Penobscot. She was brand new, with an immaculate shiny green hull and beautiful wooden thwarts and seats. We still have her now, and I doubt we will ever let her go, but she is showing signs of having been through some hard times. Once a beautifully manicured bowling green, she now resembles the grassed-over remains of a shell-scarred battlefield.

In canoeing, I was on a steep learning curve, but it was great. A whole world of unexplored rivers, lakes and seas was unfolding for me. Our first outing in our Penobscot was on the Calder and Hebble Navigation, a narrow canal and a legacy of the industrial revolution, which passes close to our

Yorkshire home. We had no clue how to keep the boat going in a straight line, slowly zig-zagging and bumping our way along, but laughing out loud and loving every second. A few days later, John, a canoeist friend from work, accompanied us to Pugneys Watersports Centre. Here, he demonstrated the basics of steering to us, and how to re-enter the canoe in the event of a capsize.

I learned to paddle on different types of water, from flowing rivers with exciting rapids to open expanses of lakes, lochs and sea.

I recalled days from my youth when Mr Taylor would train hard in the school gym for the Devizes to Westminster International Canoe Race (known as 'The DW'). This is a gruelling 125-mile non-stop time trial starting from the small town of Devizes in Wiltshire and finishing under Westminster Bridge in London. This kind of challenge greatly appealed to me, and, in 2011, just a few short months after buying our first canoe, John agreed to do the race with me.

We found training together difficult as John had a busy work and domestic life. I trained hard in the gym and paddled the canoe with Katrina as much as possible.

At the time of the race, we were experiencing the hottest Easter on record, with temperatures in London reaching almost 27 degrees Celsius. John and I set off in a heavy, non-racing canoe along the Kennet and Avon canal. We worked hard – at each lock, we would jump out of the boat as quickly as possible, put it on our shoulders and run to the next get-in point. We carried on like this, but, gradually, the heat took its toll. 35 miles in, and John was struggling. From the vacant expression on his face, I could see that he was ill. We arrived at the halfway point at Dreadnought Reach on the Thames, but John was suffering from dehydration and could not go any further. Disappointed, we retired from the race.

During the race, though, we were overtaken by a number of tandem racing kayaks – K2s. I remember looking at these streamlined boats, effortlessly gliding through the water as they passed us. I thought, 'I'll do it in one of those next time … it'll be much easier!' How wrong I was. The next five years saw me competing in this superb race not in a canoe but in a racing kayak. I also competed, at a modest level, in local and regional races.

As much as I loved the physical fitness involved in kayak racing, I drifted away from competitions. I found that I would work hard for a race and then be disappointed because I didn't do as well as I'd hoped. I never found this with recreational canoeing, which was just about having a good time on my own terms.

The sea offered endless possibilities for adventure and, with a sea loch on our doorstep in Strontian, I was captivated. Here, on Loch Sunart, with tides, waves and exposure to the weather, I learned how to paddle a canoe.

I found my thoughts continually drifting back to my early teens, paddling with Bill Taylor, and to his accomplishments in circumnavigating the UK and Ireland in a sea kayak. I began to wonder if anyone had done it in a canoe.

Some big coastal expeditions had been undertaken – notably, Ray Goodwin's circumnavigation of Wales in 1992 with Rob Egelstaff and his crossing of the Irish Sea with Dave Howe in 1994. More recently, Gavin Millar undertook a 1000-mile coastal journey in a specialised sailing canoe in 2012. No one, however, had been around the whole of the UK in a traditional open canoe.

The seeds sown in my mind in 1986 were starting to take root. I planned to attempt a circumnavigation in 2017, following my retirement from the police.

4

Fools and Tools

Circumnavigating the UK was going to be a tough challenge. I considered doing it solo, but common sense told me that going tandem would give me better odds of success. Sharing the workload, meant that more distance could be covered each day – not to mention the fact that it would be much safer being at sea as a team of a two, than alone. My first choice of partner for an adventure of any kind would always be Katrina.

'*Colin asked me if I would do the circumnavigation of the UK with him. I was tempted – it would be an amazing achievement. But it was going to be hard, both physically and mentally, and deep down I knew I didn't want it badly enough. Besides, who would take care of our two dogs, Tyke and Gonzo, if I were to join Colin in the canoe for up to five months? No – I would support him in whatever way I could from dry land, but he would have to find someone else to join him for this one.*'

With Katrina declining my invitation, I ran through the names in my head of all the canoeists I knew who might be capable of making the trip with me. I could think of a few – but would they be able to give up the necessary time, and would we be compatible in a canoe together for up to five months? Then I had a crazy idea. Davis, my nephew, would be 25 years old when I retired. He was young, fit and healthy, with an appetite for adventure. We had climbed together before, including a nine-day ascent of Muir Wall on El Capitan in Yosemite. Our compatibility in extreme circumstances had already been tested.

In 2010, Davis was 18 years old and already a passionate climber. We lay in our sleeping bags, with only the thin fabric of the portaledge tent hanging from the side of the cliff separating us from the abyss that fell 2,500 feet to the pines of the valley below. Over the previous eight days we had climbed up a vertical face of perfectly smooth granite, hauling all our food and equipment with us. Thin vertical cracks provided a tenuous path, leading us slowly towards the summit. My hands hadn't fared well with the rough Yosemite granite. They throbbed and ached, bloody from days of hard climbing. But our mood was good, and we laughed at our lack of imagination as we ate our staple meals of cheese and tortilla wraps. One more day would see us at the top.

I was aware from this experience that Davis and I were well-matched, certainly in mental attitude if not in paddling ability. With youth on his side, he was physically stronger than me. Davis had just returned from a climbing expedition to the summits of Kilimanjaro and Mount Elbrus, and was looking for his next adventure. I sent him a message, and, without hesitation, he accepted the challenge.

Happy with my choice of partner, I turned my attention to making sure we had the right equipment. The first thing was to find a canoe.

The earliest known craft of this sort, dating back to the early Mesolithic period, was found in the small village of Pesse in the Netherlands. Made from a hollowed-out Scots pine trunk, this dugout canoe was similar to others found in Scotland on the Clyde and Tay rivers. These were probably used in sheltered waters, but a glance at the Polynesians, who made thousand-mile journeys across the Pacific Ocean in outrigger canoes, gives an insight into what could be possible.

Between the dugout and the outrigger canoe, there is a middle ground, represented at its finest by the birch bark canoe of the indigenous people of Canada and North America. It was a canoe similar to this that we needed, but made from modern materials.

The Old Town Penobscot with which I had shared so many adventures wasn't quite right for this journey. I needed to find a more suitable canoe – one with a stiffer hull which was able to ride the waves and sail well, while also carrying enough equipment for a prolonged expedition.

I enlisted Katrina to undertake a research project – something she loves as it involves tables and spreadsheets. The brief was simple – find the most seaworthy canoe possible, at least 17 feet in length. After some thorough detective work, Katrina found the perfect boat – a Swift Temagami, made in Canada and named after a remote Canadian lake and river system. Although the canoe was made of Kevlar and not birch bark, it would be recognised by the aboriginal tribes of Canada as being close to their design.

Our canoe was delivered to us in April 2016 – a beautiful red and white craft with stunning ash gunwales and thwarts. We christened her Ruby. The next step was to prepare her for sailing.

~~~

A good friend from my climbing days was a keen sailor. He would regularly charter a yacht and head off into the seas and oceans. I once asked him what attracted him to sailing. I have never forgotten his response:

'It's magic. You're at the helm, alone, it's night, there's a good wind in your sails as you navigate by the stars. You're in charge, riding a mythical beast that is pounding through the waves, and all you can hear is boom ... boom ... boom, as the bow breaks through the waves. It's magic.'

Our first experience of sailing a canoe involved Katrina putting two paddle shafts inside a jacket and holding it up, allowing the wind, which was coming from behind us, to gently push the boat forwards while I used another paddle as a rudder. This provided us with a very basic sail. The only problem with this type of sailing is that you are completely at the mercy of the wind and can only go in one direction – downwind.

A little research led me to discover Solway Dory, a company in the Lake District that specialises in sailing canoes. It was owned and run by 'the two Daves', Dave Stubbs and Dave Poskitt, oracles of canoe sailing. On their advice, we bought our first proper sailing rig, which would enable us to sail upwind.

Kitted out with our new rig and a homemade rudder and leeboard (a pivoting keel attached to the side of the canoe), we headed to Coniston Water in the Lake District on a cold, dull and windy day in March 2011.

200 metres from the shore, a gust of wind caught the sail and I capsized. After a breathtakingly cold swim, I made it back to the shore, shivering and making a mental note to buy a drysuit. Wearing one of these would later turn capsizing from a hypothermic nightmare to a fun learning experience.

And so, I learned to sail a canoe. Bouncing along waves, sitting on the side of the canoe, leaning back against nothing but air to stop the boat from tipping, I was in charge of a wild steed amongst a sea of white horses.

I learned that, to make faster progress, I could help the boat along by paddling at the same time as sailing, a technique with the imaginative name of paddle-sailing. The possibility of using this technique epitomises the canoe's versatility, representing the best of both worlds, and would be essential for any big expedition.

~~~

We took the canoe to Solway Dory's workshop in Cumbria and left her there. A few weeks later, we returned to find her sporting new sailing thwarts, mast feet, a leeboard and rudder attachments, as well as wooden side rails to make hiking out more comfortable than sitting on the very narrow gunwales.

I decided to sail the canoe as a ketch, with two sails – a larger sail at the front as a mainsail and a smaller 'mizzen' sail at the rear. This would offer a degree of flexibility.
Should the wind be too strong for both sails, I could use one, and, should one become damaged, I would always have a spare. My preference was for a type of sail known as a lugsail, which can be raised or dropped quickly with the pull of a cord and has a relatively low centre of effort, thus not putting too much stress on the hull of the boat.

I imagine that some people might consider the use of sails as cheating. This might be the case if I wasn't honest and open about their use. One great thing about canoeing for me is being able to work with the wind and make the best of a free, natural resource. It seemed foolish to paddle a canoe on an expedition such as ours without accepting this helping hand from nature.

With the canoe rigged, all we needed was a couple of paddles each. Since 2015, Katrina and I had been using exquisite wooden blades from Downcreek Paddles, lovingly handcrafted by Jude and Bill Todd. I love the feel of a wooden paddle, and I was keen to use these on the trip. We placed an order with Jude for two of their new bent-shaft paddles and a traditional beaver-tail for Davis.

Six weeks before the start of the UK circumnavigation, we received these amazing examples of fine craftsmanship. With stunning lines, fine edges and a wonderfully smooth finish, they looked as though they should be displayed on a wall rather than used in a canoe.

Everything was coming together, but one thing concerned me. A canoe is open, and there is no deck to shed water. The prospect always exists that, when at sea, with waves splashing over the sides, the canoe could fill completely, and no amount of bailing would prevent this. I needed to find a remedy to address a situation like this.

We fitted six large, and two smaller, buoyancy bags to the canoe in the bow, stern, sides and centre. Our luggage was to be stowed in plastic barrels, secured into the boat with straps to add further buoyancy. With these in place, the canoe could still be paddled even when full of water. Katrina also made some simple fabric decks to cover the bow and centre of the boat and thus help to shed water, but I was keen for the canoe to remain as open as possible, so the seating area was not covered.

Our final defence against the water involved two five-litre plastic petrol cans with their ends sawn off, to be used as bailing buckets. Frantic work with these, along with a small hand-operated stirrup pump, would quickly empty a full canoe.

Both Katrina and I were very keen to use this trip as an opportunity to support a local charity. A good paddling friend, John Gilbert, had connections with the Forget Me Not children's hospice, based in Huddersfield. When we looked into this further, we realised that we could use our trip to raise money to help children who would never be able to have adventures like ours. We contacted the charity to let them know that we would use our expedition to raise funds for them.

We were almost ready to go, but I still had to complete my time in the police.

5

Final Preparation

As if I was stepping out of a 27-year marriage where neither party wanted to split, I hadn't anticipated how difficult my retirement from the police would be. I had looked forward to it for so long and had grand plans, but it was a time of upheaval and mixed emotions.

My identity, the peg from which I hung my coat, was gone. I immediately lost a lot of friends. I missed the daily buzz of work, my colleagues and the community for which I worked. But I also realised how fortunate I was to be able to retire at 49 years of age and have the opportunity to do something different. Within days of my retirement, Katrina and I moved up to our house in Strontian. The void left in my life by the police was filled with anticipation and preparation for 'The Big Trip'.

Communication with Davis wasn't easy. He was often away on climbing expeditions or visiting his girlfriend, who lived abroad. He was struggling to commit to a firm date when he would be able to leave his job and come to Scotland. I worried that he wasn't going to be able to make the trip, leaving me without a partner. Eventually, Davis confirmed that he would fly to Scotland on 24th April, just six days before our planned departure date. The clock was ticking, and I was concerned that we hadn't had enough time together to prepare. Davis had only spent a total of 11 days in a canoe up to this point.

I had wanted to paddle with Davis before we left and do some last-minute training on the sea, but there was still a lot to do. We managed just two afternoons – one on Loch Sunart, where we practised capsize recovery with a loaded canoe, and the other on the powerful white waters of the Falls of Lora.

In Davis's absence, Katrina and I rigged out the canoe and worked out how best to stow equipment. We took the boat on test paddles, checked waterproof bags and barrels for watertightness, divided food into portions, and tried out tents and shelters. We purchased high-quality specialist clothing from Peak UK, including drysuits, buoyancy aids, jackets and trousers. I was keen that Davis and I should use the same equipment.

Electronic devices, including a VHF radio, a GPS and an electronic tracking device called a Spot Messenger, were bought and tested. We printed and laminated over 200 Ordnance Survey maps of the UK coastline. These were duly sorted into stages and packed in folders, along with the relevant tidal information and notes of any particular hazards.

The overall plan was that Davis and I would set off with enough supplies to be self-sufficient for five days, camping and cooking for ourselves along the way. After this, Katrina would meet us in the van and re-supply us with food, clean clothes and fresh batteries for our electronic devices. This cycle was to continue until we finished the trip.

We hoped to take between three and five months to travel around the UK, depending on the weather. Deep down, and somewhat optimistically, I wanted to complete the trip in less than 100 days. I had read that this was considered a good amount of time for sea kayakers to complete a UK circumnavigation.

I had also read of a sea kayaker who had come up with a 'code of ethics', which laid out the 'rules' by which he would abide on his journey. I liked this idea, and so I did the same.

Only paddles and sails were to be used to provide propulsion – there would be no motorised backup or support vessels. We would use the tidal streams to our advantage and, where possible, avoid paddling at night. Our canoe would not have fixed decks, only small fabric spray decks across the bow and centre of the boat, with the cockpits remaining open. Our canoe would not be fitted with outriggers. We would circumnavigate the whole of the mainland without shortcuts. This meant that we would not use any inland canals or portage over any headlands. We would not have any prolonged breaks unless these were dictated by illness, injury or weather.

Our departure was to be from my home village of Strontian. Setting off along Loch Sunart until we reached the Atlantic Ocean, we would keep moving clockwise around the UK until we closed the circle. We aimed to travel fast and light. The weather would dictate our days off.

Our seating positions in the canoe were important and distinct. The person at the stern (rear) of the boat would maintain our course, sailing the canoe and paddling all at the same time. The person at the bow (front) would be the workhorse whose main job was to paddle, navigate and bail when necessary. At sea, the bow paddler would also be hit by more waves, a potentially cold, frightening and soul-destroying experience.

Ideally, we wanted to swap positions to add variety. However, Davis had been absent in the configuration of the boat, and there was no time for him to hone his sailing skills. I therefore made the decision that I would maintain the stern seat (helm) for the entire journey.

~~~

Six days before the start of The Big Trip, I drove to Glasgow to pick up Davis from the airport. On the way back to Strontian, we stopped off on Rannoch Moor, near Loch Tulla, at a tree which appears to grow out of a rock, with no apparent soil for its roots.

In 2004, I drove past this tree with a climbing friend, when she raised her hands in the air and bowed down.

'Hey, Angela, what are you doing?', I enquired, confused by her bizarre behaviour.

'I'm paying homage to the tree,' she said, as though this were normal. 'I've been coming to Scotland since I was a child. That tree has always been there, growing magically out of the rock. I pay homage for good luck.'

Since then, whenever I pass the tree, I also pay homage to it. On one occasion, I had a hitchhiker in the car. Goodness only knows what he thought.

This time, wanting to pay the fullest of respects, Davis and I alighted from the car and walked to the base of the rock. Kneeling on the wet grass, we bowed down to the tree. This might be a silly superstition, but, with the trip lying ahead of us, any help we could get was welcome.

I was relieved that Davis had finally arrived in Scotland. But. with his lack of involvement in the preparation for the trip, I had begun to see him as a passenger – someone I needed to complete the trip – and not as an equal.

Looking back, I regret not discussing my frustrations with Davis, but I feared that he might walk away, leaving me without a partner, so I continued as though everything was fine. Further down the line, as things became hard and stressful, festering, unaired feelings were often close to the surface. For the majority of the time we were good buddies, but there were moments when tensions between us ran high. I didn't see it at first, but, as I later discovered, the pressures on Davis were also considerable.

My lack of communication with Davis meant that I didn't understand his predicament. Just days before the trip he had split up with his girlfriend – he had sacrificed his job working in an outdoor shop in Limerick in order to come on the trip, and he had given up his tenancy, leaving him homeless and his future uncertain.

Davis was 25 years old – his own man – not the inexperienced youth I had previously led in the mountains. He was as capable as I was, and it is to both our credit that we worked together, overcame differences and kept going under pressure in extreme circumstances.

6

Making History

29th April 2017: we had made our final checks of our canoe and equipment, and tomorrow we would be leaving. Our friends, Tim and Lynn, the owners of Sunart Camping, had agreed that we could use the barbeque facilities at the campsite for a farewell get-together. Many of our friends and family members had travelled up to Scotland to see us off on our adventure.

It was a pleasant evening, but Davis and I were restless. We had a long journey ahead of us, and we wanted to get going. Hanging over me was the knowledge that Davis and I were about to put ourselves to a severe test. While I put on a brave face, I had no idea how we would fare against some of the obstacles which lay ahead: Cape Wrath, the Pentland Firth, Flamborough Head, Dover, Portland Bill and the Pembrokeshire coast to name but a few. Research into any one of these would be enough to put some people off making the journey we were going to make in a 40-foot yacht, let alone in a tiny canoe. Then there were big ships, which I had never really come across and with which I was soon to become well acquainted. Katrina's uncle, an experienced merchant seaman, stressed on hearing about our adventures that we should, 'Watch out for ships, they can't stop, and they can't see you.'

Above all, I was worried about Davis. We hadn't trained as much as I had hoped, yet we were about to embark on a massive adventure and he had only spent 12 days in a canoe to prepare.

The following morning, the day of departure, we were lucky. A strong wind was blowing, but, fortunately, it was coming from the east, assisting our voyage up Loch Sunart on the first leg of our journey. Had the wind been the prevailing westerly, we would have had to postpone our start.

It was time to go. After stuffing a bacon butty provided by the Strontian Hotel into my mouth and the exchange of hugs all around, we spun the canoe like professionals and paddled away. A happy collection of kayakers from the Pennine Canoe Club and some others in a fishing boat escorted us away. It was a relief to get going and leave everything behind. All that mattered now was what lay ahead. Davis and I nervously began to acquaint ourselves with the canoe. Pushed by a good wind, we surfed the boat along white caps for 23 miles to Kilchoan, where we would finish our first leg.

We were both in good spirits. I shouted, 'Hey, Davis, we're making canoeing history!'

It was hard to imagine that, in three months, we would be back on Loch Sunart, heading in the opposite direction, going home.

~~~

Kilchoan, the most westerly village in the UK, is one of my favourite places. Surrounded by mountains, until 1900 it was only accessible by boat. There is a wonderful feeling there of being at a crossroads, at the edge of something bigger. Your eyes rest easy on far-ranging views – to the east, Loch Sunart, to the south the Sound of Mull. In the distance, to the west, the islands of Coll and Tiree lie remote and windswept in the Atlantic Ocean.

I have always felt at home and welcomed by the villagers in Kilchoan. As in many places in remote areas of the west coast of Scotland, multi-tasking represents the only way to earn a living wage. It's not unusual for a person to work three or four small jobs to make ends meet. There is a sense of community not found in bigger towns, where people look after each other. It was the perfect place to stop for our first night.

Graham, our affable friend and neighbour from Strontian, had driven out to Kilchoan in his campervan to meet us and cook our tea that evening. In his younger days, living in Glasgow, he had been a hill walker and climber on the periphery of the notorious Creagh Dhu Mountaineering Club. From his work in hard rock mining and forestry, and later employment as an electrician on hydroelectric schemes, Graham had stories to tell. In later years, he took his love of adventurous exploits into sailing. He entertained us with tales of whisky-fuelled crossings on the high seas. He was also a superb ship's cook, and his pasta that evening was delicious.

After tea, we spent our first night on the floor of a small windswept boathouse beside the jetty. The boathouse was equipped as a gym for locals, so we moved a few weights about to make enough room to sleep – the exercise mats made excellent beds.

The alarm went off at 4 am. In our state of excitement, getting up was easy. The wind was gusting too strongly, and a quick walk outside to look at the sea confirmed that we would have to wait. We were in no rush, though. Graham cooked breakfast, and, 45 minutes later, after the wind had settled to a steady force 4 breeze, we pushed out into the royal blue sea.

Compared to the previous day, conditions were calm as we paddle-sailed around the cliffs of the Ardnamurchan peninsula and out towards the Isle of Eigg. It was a couple of hours before I realised that I'd forgotten to switch on our tracking device, the Spot Messenger. This was no more than a minor oversight, but I was angry with myself. The error was a measure of my state of mind and the pressure I was feeling. Hundreds of people were following our progress on a live link, and I felt foolish. To make things worse, Davis didn't say anything about it.

The Isle of Eigg, overlooked by the magnificent cliffs of An Sgurr, was our first stop as we waited for the tide to turn. I shelved the Spot Messenger mistake in my mind, took photographs and relaxed. It was a glorious, still, sunny day. The next tide saw us in a still, calm sea, paddling across to the Isle of Skye where we stopped for the night.

Pitching a tarp on a salt marsh is always risky as, at certain high tides, such marshes can become submerged. We looked at the surrounding lines of seaweed and guessed that the one we were on would be ok. I began to prepare tea – lentil curry.

A friend had given me a suggestion for cooking lentil curry outdoors. I should first bring the lentils to the boil for just a few minutes, and then wrap the pan in a sleeping bag to insulate it. This would allow the lentils to continue cooking while I used the stove to boil the rice. Heeding this advice, I duly wrapped the boiling pan of lentils in my sleeping bag while I continued to cook the rice.

Ten minutes into this process, Davis popped his head out from under the tarp and called over to me, 'Err, Colin … I think the curry has spilt.'

I hurried under the tarp and peeled back the hood of my sleeping bag. 'Oh, no!'

Half the contents of the pan were swilling around in the spot where my head was soon supposed to be. It looked like the contents of a baby's nappy … and it didn't smell much better. I cleaned my bag as best as I could, but, for weeks to come, I caught the pungent whiff of curry while drifting off to sleep. To this day, I still can't stand the smell of cardamom.

I soon realised that I had misjudged the type of food we would need for this venture. I had planned to eat healthily. Our main meals would consist of lentil curry with rice, Beanfeast with pasta and TVP (textured vegetable protein) with couscous and dried vegetables. Snacks would be high in calories and include muesli bars and cheese. I had spent weeks drying out fruit. I wanted to avoid junk food as much as possible. Within days of starting the hard physical work of the journey, both Davis and I craved fatty food, especially sausages and pizza. The dried fruit was good, but we heavily supplemented this with chocolate bars and flapjack.

As far as food went, we had got one thing right though. A month before our departure, Graham had taken delivery of a large parcel for us. He was curious, and, when I collected it from him, I explained that it was 14 kg of instant custard powder. Jokingly, I told him it was good for my skin. I'm not sure he got this. I dread to think of the rumours going around the village. Instant custard and Pop Tarts were our go-to staples for pudding.

7

Surf's Up

2nd – 4th May 2017

Paddling onwards in hot, still conditions, we made it to Kyle Rhea, the narrow channel separating Skye from the mainland. Our passage through here was much less dramatic than it had been two years previously on our circumnavigation of Skye. Catching the north-flowing tidal stream, we arrived at the Skye Bridge as the sun was setting and made camp for the night. After just a few hours' sleep, an inspiring sunrise welcomed us on the first tide.

A calm start quickly became a rough and bumpy ride, past fishing boats rocking animatedly in the choppy swell. After a few miles, the wind eased and the sea became smooth. Our speed decreased, and paddling was our only way forward. For several hours along the Inner Sound, between the mainland and the island of Raasay, we had a stalker. Eerily, about a kilometre behind, a submarine was following us, and I couldn't help but think that they were monitoring our progress.

Our midway landing point for the day was a tropical-looking, deserted, white sandy beach. The submarine maintained its ominous presence in the distance, and my paranoia increased by the minute. The beach was to be our base for a few hours until the next tide, but it was here that the trip nearly ended for me.

As the water I was heating on the camping stove came to a rolling boil, the kettle became unstable and tipped over. My bare feet were in the path of the boiling water. I swore, howled and ran into the cold sea. I was fortunate, however, and suffered only minor scalding. A couple of inches closer and my injuries would have been more severe. Sometimes, a very fine line exists between success and failure. Disaster is never far away.

We continued silently northwards under clear blue May skies, surrounded by a superb mountainous coastline interspersed with quiet bays, deep lochs and the occasional sandy beach. Paddling and sailing for most of the time, I felt myself getting fitter, and Davis and I were both becoming more confident in the canoe.

The swell picked up as we headed towards the Summer Isles, a small archipelago of little islands, beautiful and remote. At first, we rode over the waves as though they were gentle speed bumps, but, steadily, they grew in size. As the swell increased, so did our anxiety. We felt vulnerable, always hoping that the next wave wouldn't be any bigger. The energy in the sea was palpable and growing by the second.

The wind had shifted to a northerly and the swell was now even more threatening. We were forced to tack into the headwind, but our efforts proved futile as the wind and swell joined forces against us and prevented any progress. I hoped, with halting breath, that the waves wouldn't start to break as our boat fell into the shadow of each oncoming swell. Our only option was to head for shore. We searched both maps and the horizon for possibilities of where to land. To our right, about half a mile away, we could see a sandy beach. Knowing full well that the swell causing us problems here would magnify considerably as it rolled onto the beach as surf, we changed course and headed for it with blinkered optimism borne out of necessity.

By now I was extremely nervous. I could see wave after wave heading for the beach, rising and turning into big breaking surf. Landing here, we would be putting ourselves in harm's way, but we had little choice. Some distance off the shore, we stopped and surveyed the scene, looking for the best place to come ashore.

With a sense of urgency, we took down both masts and stowed them away, along with everything else that could be swept off the boat. This was made more difficult as the canoe was rising and falling on the swell, which hurried underneath us. Raising our voices to hear each other over the din of the crashing waves, we decided on the safest point to land, away from rocks protruding into the sea from the right-hand side of the beach.

Like timid men being pushed into a fight, we slowly made our way to our fate. The palpable, and likely, risk was that a big wave would capsize us, spinning us into the water as though we were in a gigantic washing machine.

The canoe lurched forwards as a wave passed underneath us. We watched as it continued on its journey towards the beach. A long, thin white line stretched out in front of us as the wave started to curl at the edge and break into an avalanche of white water. The same happened with the next wave, and the next. With the resignation of a convict on death row, I knew that it was only a matter of time before we would become victims of mother nature. Then it came.

The rear of the canoe lifted into the air. The wave propelled us forward, too fast for me to control. I was unable to keep the boat in a straight line.

Whoosh! The wave broke, and in a second we were thrown from the boat into the water, crashing and spinning. In the foam, everything around us turned white, and we were swept to shore along with the heavy, swamped canoe. Coughing, spluttering and struggling against the continuing onslaught of water, we pulled the boat past the last line of retreating surf. A quick check revealed that we were both ok, and the canoe was intact. We had got away with it. I looked at Davis, and, together, we burst out laughing.

There was not so much as a footprint in the golden sand or the slightest sign of human activity. The isolated, lonely beach, surrounded by steep banks and cliffs, felt very remote. Now, we were on an adventure. With the decision already made for us to stop here, we looked for a campsite.

The only piece of flat land not covered in sand was some distance away from the canoe, up a steep, grassy, terraced slope. Carrying our heavy equipment was a chore, made worse by the necessity of passing a stinking, maggot-ridden, dead seal.

Before going to bed, I climbed up a steep sheep track to the edge of the cliffs surrounding the beach and broke the solitude by making a phone call to Katrina while watching the sunset cast its orange glow on the horizon.

Five days into our journey, and we had been through our first test. With so little opportunity to paddle together beforehand, we had never practised surf landings. Despite the ungracious dunking, we were both happy with how things had gone. Little did we know that, just two weeks later, we would face surf waves again, and this time it would threaten to put an end to the expedition.

8

Lessons and Encounters

5th – 8th May 2017

We were starting to settle into a routine and develop strategies to make life easier along the way. In the confined space of the canoe, keeping things tidy yet accessible was important. We always had an individual small flask of hot coffee each and some snacks close to hand, along with other essentials such as sun cream, sunglasses, lip balm and spare clothing.

Each day, we updated the coastguard with our plans and activated the Spot Messenger before paddling for five to six hours, sometimes longer, depending on the tidal flow. When we arrived at each destination, we updated the coastguard of our safe arrival and turned off the Spot Messenger before checking the weather forecast, maps and tidal charts, and deciding on our next objective.

I began to look forward to the first break of the day, which usually happened after about an hour of paddling. We tended to drift for ten minutes, drink coffee and eat biscuits or dried fruit. After this, we stopped for five minutes every hour for a quick break. But all of this was dependent on conditions. There was no stopping when the going was tough.

Over the next few days, the winds set in from a northerly direction, straight into our faces. To make any progress at all required a combination of sailing and hard paddling. In these early days, we paddled in conditions which, later, we would have avoided. Sometimes the distance gained isn't worth the energy or risk. Both Davis and I were losing weight from physical exertion. It wasn't uncommon for us to land soaked in sweat and encrusted in salt.

We paddled most of the time, even when the wind was helping us. Only when there was a chance of capsizing did I stop paddling and concentrate on the sails.

Davis was the stronger paddler of the two of us and had a unique, dynamic paddle stroke. Like a miner at a coalface, he attacked the water with his paddle, reaching forward and plunging his blade into the sea. He used all of his strength to pull back hard. When Davis paddled, I felt obliged to do the same. I learned to control the tiller bar, paddle and sail simultaneously, stopping only to bail when water sploshed around my feet. In these early days, Davis's work rate was a cause for concern and a minor irritation for me. I got the impression that he didn't really want to be there and just wanted to finish the job quickly. I should have talked to him about it, but I didn't, not wanting to elicit a negative response.

On a steep learning curve, we set off on our second leg of the day from one of the small islands of the Summer Isles. This day was to be a school day.

The strong northerly wind blowing against the flow of the tide made for small but steep, white-capped waves. Keen to make progress, we considered our options and decided that we would be able to paddle-sail. We launched into a sea from which we should have walked away.

The wind was too powerful for our big mainsail, causing the boat to heel violently and continually threatening to capsize us. Sheltering in the lee of a small island, we replaced the mainsail with the smaller mizzen. We hoped that this would allow us to paddle while still gaining some advantage from the wind. However, this sail was too small to be useful. We couldn't generate enough power to counteract the combined force of the wind and the waves against the hull of the boat. We were being blown sideways and backwards.

From my head down, I was soaked with cold spray. Water was coming into the canoe from all angles. Waves broke over the gunwales and flooded into the boat. Water surged over the bow as the canoe buried itself in the waves.

We felt no fear, but experienced an undercurrent of anxiety. I was bailing with one hand and steering with the other and, after several buckets of water had been ditched into the sea, I paddled. Making headway was virtually impossible and, after five hours of non-stop, frantic action, we had managed to cover a distance of only two miles.

Our spirits were almost crushed and, just as we thought things couldn't get much worse, the tide turned against us. We ground on and managed to limp into the small harbour of Old Dornie, the nearest place available to land. The air was filled with the pungent smell of rotting crabs and fish as we pitched our tent beside old fishing boats and creels. We were shattered.

Thankfully, the wind eased overnight, and an early start saw us making good progress. We stopped for a minute, taking in the spectacular sandstone monolith of the Old Man of Stoer. From here, we had to undertake an 11-mile crossing to get to our next goal – the small village of Scourie.

We chatted briefly about our options. While we didn't say much, we knew that the strength of the headwind was due to increase and the tidal flow would turn against us in a few hours.

The only bonus for us was that having the wind and tide in the same direction would mean a flatter sea.

'Are we doing this, Davis?'

'Yeah.'

So we began. The predicted conspiracy of elements turned what could have been a beautiful, leisurely paddle into another momentous struggle. Unbeknown to us, as we approached Scourie, Katrina was filming us as we frantically bailed buckets of water over the side of the canoe before continuing to paddle.

The calm, clear shallow waters of Scourie Bay were a delight. Katrina was on the beach, and Tyke and Gonzo left her side, charging into the sea and barking with delight, giving us a welcome which only dogs are capable of.

With strong winds forecast for the following day, we had no choice but to have a day off and wait for better conditions. We joined Katrina in the van, where we relaxed and checked maps and weather forecasts.

It was a warm, sunny day, and we had left the rear and side doors of the van open to let some air flow through. We had magnetic signs on the outside of the van showing the logo we had used for the Canoe Around Britain website and details of the Forget Me Not children's hospice, for which we were raising funds.

As we chilled out inside the van, I heard a familiar deep Yorkshire voice from outside, 'Is that the Forget Me Not charity from Huddersfield?'

I jumped out of the van, and, sure enough, there stood my ex-work colleague, friend and fellow canoeist Simon Spencer and his wife, Angela. I hadn't seen Simon for a few years. We chatted and, of course, drank Yorkshire Tea. This chance encounter turned out to be great for morale.

We left Scourie early the next morning, waving goodbye to Simon, Angela and Katrina. The forecast was not great, but the sheltered bay at Scourie led us into a false sense of security.

On entering the open sea, reality hit us in the form of a strong headwind. What followed was a five-hour, ten-mile battle against the wind to our next stop, a small, but perfectly formed white, sandy beach.

The beach was stunning, but I was unable to appreciate the magnificence of my surroundings. The destination was becoming more important than the journey, and the arduous circumstances were a major distraction from the scenery. Only later, when I think back and look at photos, could I appreciate where we were, in one of the most beautiful places in the world.

We were exhausted and burdened with the realisation that the UK is a big island, and we were only a fraction of the way into our journey. Canoeing around the whole thing was going to be much harder than we had thought.

On this beach, Davis started to open up and talk about some personal issues that were playing on his mind. He spoke of his relationship that had broken down just days before our trip, and the fact that he didn't know where he was going to live when he got back home. To cap it all, he had just learned that a good friend of his had died in tragic circumstances.

The challenge we had embarked upon was hard enough without the heavy burden of domestic problems he was carrying. It is to my regret that I didn't speak to Davis more about his welfare and how he was doing other than the usual 'You ok, mate?' The truth is, I was afraid that he would tell me he needed to get back home, and the trip would be over.

9

North to East

9th May 2017

Cape Wrath is a bombing range used by the RAF. It was also the first significant milestone of our journey – the point where we would stop travelling north, and turn to the east.

From a hill overlooking our beach – the only place where I could get a mobile signal – I had spoken to the range controller. The range would be active first thing in the morning, but we would be able to pass through after 11 am. This was both good and bad: good because we would be turning the corner the following day, bad because the tidal stream along the north coast was due to be flowing westwards from 11 am.

~~~

The coming and going of the tide is a magnificent event that happens daily, like the rising sun and the changing moon.

During my first excursions into the sea, I didn't understand the nature of tides and dismissed them almost entirely. All that mattered to me was how far up the beach the water would rise, and, in turn, how far I needed to carry my canoe so that it wouldn't be washed away while I camped. If the tide turned against me while I was out at sea, I would have to paddle harder. Looking back at those early forays, I laugh at my naivety.

For anyone looking to learn about tides, I recommend *The Book of Tides* by William Thomson, although I wouldn't advocate reading this just before embarking on a major coastal journey by canoe, as it might scare the wits out of you before you even begin.

In simple terms, the alignment of the moon to the earth, with its gravitational pull, and, to a lesser extent, the sun's gravity, drive the tides. On an almost bi-weekly basis, when a full moon or a new moon occurs, the pull is strong, creating big spring tides (where the difference in water height between low tide and high tide is at its greatest). In between these times, when a half moon occurs, the gravitational pull is less, causing weaker neap tides.

What most people see and understand of tides is that water comes further up the beach as the tide comes in and recedes further as the tide goes out. This is only a fraction of the story. As well as rising and falling, water continually flows around the coast in predictable patterns known as the tidal stream. During spring tides, tidal streams can flow up to twice as fast as during neap tides.

On one of Katrina's and my early coastal canoe trips, we planned to sail along the west coast of Scotland from Glenuig to Mallaig, where our intention was to go to the best fish and chip shop we know for tea – a distance which should easily be covered in a day. We set off, completely oblivious to what the tide was doing. The wind was coming from in front of us, so we had to tack but we couldn't understand why any progress was so pitiful. Eventually, we gave up on trying to sail and decided to move closer to shore and just paddle. After what seemed like an eternity, we landed in Mallaig … well after closing time at the chippy.

Only in 2015, at the Open Canoe Association's Canoefest in North Wales, did Katrina and I learn about tidal flows, as we paddled on the Menai Strait with experienced canoeists. We realised then that we had been trying to reach Mallaig against the flow, like going the wrong way on a moving walkway at the airport. We learned that, to get somewhere without a struggle, we had to know the direction in which the tidal streams were flowing.

Some tidal streams, especially on neap tides, can be barely noticeable, while others flow like fast-moving rivers. It is usual to catch the short ferry over the Corran Narrows in the tidal Loch Linnhe to reach our village of Strontian. Here, on a spring tide, you would be forgiven for thinking that you were crossing a river.

Tidal streams don't flow at a constant speed – they gradually speed up and slow down throughout their cycles. There are books available which provide this information and outline the direction and speed of the tidal stream at any time on any particular day.

When a flow of water hits obstacles, the area behind where the water flows back on itself is called an eddy. We discovered that, at sea, tidal eddies can often be found close to shore and these can be used advantageously when the main tidal stream flows against you. This brings risks. Paddling close to shore, with rocks nearby and a thumping, breaking swell crashing around, requires a cool head and good boat handling skills to avoid shipwreck.

In many places around the UK coastline, a fast-flowing tidal stream collides with an underwater obstacle or, less commonly, a tide going in the opposite direction. This causes millions of tonnes of water to be pushed up to the surface, resulting in steep, white-capped waves, sometimes as big as six metres high. This is known as a tide race, over-fall or tidal rapid. A canoe caught up in a tide race is extremely vulnerable and passing places where these races occur requires precise timing.

~~~

Now, at the north east corner of Scotland, we had no choice but to wait.

With this in mind, we began our day's journey listening to the thunder of the fighter jets doing their thing as we paddled slowly to a point one mile from Cape Wrath. We arrived a little early, and the red warning flag of the range was still flying. Taking the opportunity for a rest, we drifted for a while, eating oatcakes and cheese. At 11 am, the flag was taken down, and all was clear.

Then came a moment I will always remember. At the very tip of the UK, I could see both the north and west coasts of Scotland simultaneously. I had the feeling of being at an immense junction. The place I had seen so many times on a map was now before me, like a vast three-dimensional model. This was a wild place dominated by massive, spectacular cliffs. To our left was the endless horizon of the north Atlantic Ocean, with its untamed, colliding currents and potent seas.

We paddled hard, our strokes in time with each other, trying to make progress eastwards. The lighthouse on the clifftop did not move, and its transit remained still. Working as hard as we could but still not moving with the strong tide against us, we were stuck. Even with the wind in our sails, all of our effort was required to keep us from drifting back.

The seas were boiling and bouncy, and tidal races were forming. Intimidating, random, white caps were breaking around us with more frequency. Turning back here was unthinkable. At times like this, small things can make a huge difference. I altered the angle of the boat very slightly. The sail generated more power, and we began to creep forwards. After a one-mile slog along the north coast, Davis noticed a jetty within a deep notch in the cliffs. Slowly, and with determination, we made our way towards it to land flanked either side by broken cliffs.

Catching the late tide from our port on Cape Wrath, we headed for Durness. We had a favourable wind but the following swell steadily increased. We had just one small sail instead of two to keep our speed down. The last thing we wanted was to surf a wave, lose control and capsize a long way offshore in no man's land. We remained about a mile from the coast as the wind picked up. I felt utterly insignificant as the swell became monstrous.

The coastline of northern Scotland was relatively flat and, compared to the west coast, unremarkable, but the sea compensated for the lack of scenery. The waters here felt powerful. There was always a swell, often large, which had latent energy like a crowd at a football stadium threatening to break into enormous cheers of violent waves. It was an intimidating place.

One minute we were riding high, looking at a stunning panoramic view of the sea and land, then we would plummet into a trough. The wind would drop and sails flap as the waves sheltered the canoe like a seaside windbreak. Here, there was no horizon – the only thing visible in every direction was water.

As if this wasn't scary enough, every 20 seconds or so as we paddled towards our destination we would hear an explosion like a gunshot as a wave broke and crashed. We were playing a game of Russian roulette with the sea, waiting nervously for the wave with our name on it. It was beyond belief that we landed safely at Durness in the setting sun, relieved and happy with the day's progress.

I thought the swell that day had been in the region of six metres but wasn't sure, so asked Davis for his opinion. He looked at me, his hat crusty with salt and sweat, and, without hesitation said, '20 to 30 feet. I regularly paint houses with my Dad, and it was like standing on the roof of a two-storey house.'

The north coast of Scotland isn't particularly long. We had just turned our first corner, yet we were only a day and a half's paddling away from the next. Soon, we would have to pass through one of the most infamous stretches of water in the world, which I naively believed to be the crux of our journey ... the Pentland Firth.

10

Grounded

10th – 13th May 2017

Perched uncomfortably on the fabric of my canoe seat, I could see the white caps of the waves as they danced in the distance towards the massive peninsula of Dunnet Head. Yet another dangerous tide race to avoid. It had been a long day – we had made use of two full tides to cover almost 50 miles from Durness. Throughout our journey along Scotland's north coast, I had been nervous. It felt exposed with very few boats around. The powerful swell and the cold, dull sea never allowed me to relax.

It was dark as we pulled into the bay at Scrabster, just below the clubhouse of the Pentland Firth Yacht Club where Katrina was waiting outside in the van. We were stopping here to rest and take stock for a few days, as the weather forecast was bleak. Strong easterly winds and a spring tide meant that we were grounded.

In the morning, Davis and I pulled our canoe up the slipway and left it at the side of the clubhouse before driving to John O'Groats to meet Katrina's parents, who had made the journey from Lincolnshire to see us. I scanned the shore, looking for glimpses of the coast and any indication of what lay ahead. After a light lunch in the café, we said goodbye to Katrina's parents and travelled to Duncansby Head, where I hoped that a better view of the sea awaited us.

Grassy and windswept, Duncansby Head is at the north east corner of the UK. Looking west, you can see the north coast stretching along the Pentland Firth, past Stroma. Walking for a short distance and looking south, you see the Duncansby Stacks – huge, conical fangs of rock eroded from the main sea cliff and home to thousands of seabirds. In the distance, to the north east, are the Pentland Skerries, and further north lies the hazy outline of the Orkney Islands.

Conditions were bright and sunny, but a stiff breeze was blowing from the east. Standing beneath the impressive lighthouse, we looked out across the Pentland Firth. I have never before, or since, seen a sea like this. Hundreds of huge, dancing, pointed waves created lines of white froth. Close in, whirlpools spun between stretches of boiling water, flowing like rivers in places. I moved to various different viewpoints but everywhere the view was the same. I knew that this was not a place where a canoe could survive, or, for that matter, many other vessels. I could only hope that, when the wind calmed and the tide slowed, we would have a chance. There was no turning back now.

We returned to Scrabster in silence, full of apprehension about what was to come. On arrival at the yacht club, we found a note on our canoe. Immediately, my heart sank. We hadn't been able to contact anyone from the club to ask permission to leave the boat there, and I envisaged a written reprimand from a disgruntled Commodore. Davis climbed out of the van and picked the note off the canoe. It read as follows:

Hi,

Like your sailing canoe.

I'm just in the clubhouse at the moment if you want to say hi, or I'll be on the water.

I think the club still has an arrangement where passing through sailors can pick up a key from the Scrabster Harbour Office and use the showers in this clubhouse.

If I miss you, have a great sail. I assume you are en route.

Steve

PFYC

We entered the clubhouse and met with Steve Foster, a charismatic and energetic man. We spent some time talking about our journey and what we could expect as we continued on our way. Steve was an experienced sailor and dinghy racer, and his advice on passage through the Pentland Firth was invaluable.

The following morning, we were enjoying a much-needed lie-in when, at 9 am, we were woken by a knock at the van door. Sleepily, Davis slid the door open to find Steve standing there, bright and cheerful. 'Hi, what are you guys planning on doing today?' he asked chirpily.

'We've not thought that far ahead,' I replied, still half asleep.

'Right, we're gonna take you into Wick. We can grab a bite to eat and visit the Heritage Museum. I think you'll like it.'

'Errr, yeah, ok, that sounds good.'

'I'll come back in an hour, give you a chance to get ready.'

True to his word, Steve returned an hour later with his wife, Jane. We all piled into their car, Tyke and Gonzo included, and headed off to Wick, where we spent an enjoyable few hours in lovely company, learning about the historical role of the herring industry in the town.

Back at the clubhouse, we got talking to another sailor who had heard of our adventure. He described the Pentland Firth, as he had experienced it in his 30-foot yacht, as a gigantic egg box: 'one minute, you're on the crest of a massive wave, and the next you're plummeting into a deep hole. This is when you take on water.'

My confidence eroded further as he told us of a cargo ship that had sunk two years previously while going through the Pentland Firth, taking all its crew with it.

'But,' he said with a smile, 'time it right, and you'll be fine.'

The next day, the wind was due to drop to a steady breeze from the south west. Steve reckoned we would be good to go. Carefully studying our tidal flow charts, Davis and I calculated the best time to approach the Pentland Firth to avoid the worst of the tide races. We prepared to set off early in the morning. Our calculations gave us three hours to reach Duncansby Head.

11

The Pentland Firth

14ᵗʰ – 16ᵗʰ May 2017

As we left the bay at dawn, conditions were breezy but calm. We were heading into the unknown. I was quietly nervous, not knowing if we would survive the next leg of our journey.

Crossing the wide, calm bay to the hulking mass of Dunnet Head was easy. We paddled close to its imposing cliffs and felt the force of the tide, but there was no tide race. We continued down the other side of the headland and along the coastline. Our next obstacle was the Merry Men of Mey, a tide race that runs north from St John's Point, like Morris dancers dressed in white, tall waves dance as the tide rushes over underwater rocks. We timed our journey through these well. Boiling waters and strong currents pulled the canoe and bounced us over a few small waves of a juvenile race which I suspected would, in a few hours, develop into an unruly thug.

Shortly after rounding St John's Point, we pulled into a small sandy bay. The wind had picked up, making the canoe difficult to control, and I was worried that we had too much sail. We removed the mainsail and put the smaller mizzen in its place. Here, I was able to get a good signal on my VHF radio, so I contacted the coastguard to let them know that we were planning on paddling through the Pentland Firth in our canoe. I could hear the surprised concern in the operator's voice as they confirmed with us that we were experienced and well equipped.

'What's your destination? Over,' the coastguard asked

'Wick. Over.'

A pause followed.

'Wick harbour is closed. The swell is over two metres, and it's unsafe to land there. Over.'

I surprised even myself with my reply. 'That's not a problem. We're a canoe. We'll find somewhere to land. Over.'

Another pause ensued.

'Ok. Please keep me updated every hour. Over.'

In preparation for the ordeal to come, we both tied ourselves to a throwline attached to the canoe. We figured that it was essential that we didn't lose contact with the boat should we capsize, as it would be our only source of salvation. This was a tactic we went on to use in all potentially rough seas we encountered.

As the Duncansby headland and its lighthouse rose before us, we could see waves breaking ahead. The swell grew in size, and each wave was bigger than the last as we were pulled towards the jaws of the Duncansby Bore tide race. There was no escape: we were committed. Giant, intimidating waves came towards us, breaking randomly across our horizon.

Looking for the best route through, the line of least resistance, I called over to Davis, 'Where do you reckon, Davis?'

Davis hesitated for a second and then shouted, 'To the right looks best.'

'Ok, here we go!'

We both paddled hard, knowing that this was no place to linger. I desperately scanned my surroundings, looking for any waves about to break so that I could steer the canoe away from them. The boat slid from crest to trough through this no-man's-land of boiling water. A devastating wave broke to my right, then a similar one to the left. Either would have sunk us if they had hit us straight on. My senses were on high alert. This was no time to be scared – we were in the thick of a battle.

We rode down a huge water slide into a deep trough and could do nothing but watch as the next wave rose steeply in front of us. Then the inevitable happened. The wave broke into a mass of white water which slammed into Davis's chest and over our heads. Instantly, the canoe was filled almost to the gunwales with cold seawater, leaving us extremely unstable. I desperately wanted to stop paddling and bail water out to gain stability, but the waves kept coming, and we had no choice but to keep going. I realised that it would only take one more wave breaking over us to capsize us.

I repeatedly shouted, 'Davis ... Keep paddling ... Keep paddling!'

And we paddled.

Gradually, things calmed down. I managed to re-gain my composure, but I could see more breaking waves in our path. We bailed the canoe as quickly as we could and continued through the gauntlet. The next series of waves was the biggest yet, and I found myself holding my breath as we paddled down one side and up the next, exhaling with relief when it didn't break. We managed to steer through the worst, but we had some close calls as walls of water broke around us in mighty white caps, too close for comfort.

Eventually, after what felt like an eternity, we rounded the corner. The waves became smaller but more confused. Feeling like a naughty schoolboy, I radioed through to the coastguard to tell them that all was good as we headed south past the fairy tale Duncansby Stacks.

I was elated. We had done it. We had got through the Pentland Firth. Katrina had seen it all from the clifftops above and this is her account:

'Standing on the grassy clifftop beneath the lighthouse at Duncansby Head, I set my camcorder up on its tripod and took out my binoculars, watching anxiously for the canoe to come into view. Eventually, in the distance, I saw them – paddling boldly towards the tide race which was beginning to form in the sea below.

From my vantage point, I could see Duncansby Bore stirring, 200 metres from the cliffs. Its ominous presence was given away by the white foam atop large breaking waves. The water looked calmer close to the cliff, and, surely, this would be where Colin would steer the canoe.

As they got closer, I found myself talking, almost shouting, out loud, "Move over. You need to get closer to shore. You're too far left." Like a moth to the flame, the canoe headed straight for the centre of the race. It was clear they were heading into trouble. "You need to move right." I could do nothing but watch as waves surrounded the tiny vessel containing my husband and nephew.

For a brief moment, the canoe disappeared from sight. A wall of water rose up directly in its path and came crashing down over the top of the mast. They were still upright, and I held my breath as they slowly made their way through.'

My radio crackled into life. I was relieved to hear from the coastguard that the swell had subsided and Wick harbour had opened again.

Sitting proud like returning war heroes, we paddled into the harbour to a reception of curious mariners who had been listening to our radio communication with the coastguard.

'Are you the guys who have just come through the Pentland Firth?' one yachtsman asked in disbelief.

'Yeah, that was us.'

'In that?' He pointed at our canoe. 'Unbelievable. You had the coastguard worried,' he laughed, 'I've never heard of anyone having to give hourly updates.'

To most, it was inconceivable that a canoe had made it through the Pentland Firth, particularly on a day when they'd had to close the harbour.

The winds for the next few days were forecast to be strong easterlies. The day of our arrival was Sunday and the harbour master, who obviously thought we were mad, told us that we wouldn't be able to leave the harbour until Wednesday at the earliest. He was a man you didn't argue with. Once again, we were stuck.

Our time in Wick was mainly spent reading and visiting local historical sights, but we were restless. Inactivity is trying for busy men. Davis and I wanted to get back in the boat and head down the east coast. As we were whiling away time in the harbour at Wick, I made a phone call to Ray.

~~~

I first met Ray Goodwin in 2015. Ray has a reputation in the outdoor world that is unrivalled in the UK. His many global mountaineering and canoeing expeditions are legendary. Now in his mid-sixties, he continues to coach anyone interested in canoeing, from beginners to the experienced, but his intelligence, keen sense of humour and voice of reason have taken him to the top. Many people can handle a canoe as well as Ray. But few, within the UK, have the same breadth and depth of knowledge as him, acquired through over 40 years of adventure.

Having made the first-ever circumnavigation of Wales and the first crossing of the Irish Sea by canoe, Ray was arguably the most experienced coastal canoeist in the UK, and the ideal person to speak to about our planned adventure.

With the Outdoor Pursuits Group at
Harrisons Rocks
photographer unknown

Climbing at Stanage Edge in the Peak
District 1983
photographer unknown

Kayaking with the Outdoor Pursuits
Group
photographer unknown

Colin and Davis standing beneath El Capitan, Yosemite
photographer unknown

Davis on Muir Wall, El Capitan *photo Colin Skeath*

Preparing to launch from Strontian *photo Katrina Skeath*

Davis, waiting for the lentil curry to cook on Skye *photo Colin Skeath*

Approaching Skye Bridge at sunset *photo Colin Skeath*

Leaving from the Skye Bridge   *photo Katrina Skeath*

Preparing to leave Scourie   *photo Katrina Skeath*

Setting off from Scrabster
photo Katrina Skeath

Stills from a video of Colin and Davis going through the Pentland Firth

"Hey Davis, that's the last boat I was captain of!" off Rattray Head
photo Colin Skeath

After leaving Rattray Head   *photo Colin Skeath*

Landing in the Harbour at Gourdon *photo Katrina Skeath*

Ollie Jay and friends near the Farne Isles *photo Davis Gould-Duff*

Leaving Filey Sailing Club *photo Katrina Skeath*

Davis with his mum, Kate, enjoying a day off at Bridlington *photo Colin Skeath*

Racing a dinghy on approach to Wells-next-the-Sea
photo Davis Gould-Duff

Coming to land at the breakwaters of Happisburgh *photo Katrina Skeath*

Landing at Happisburgh *photo Katrina Skeath*

Katrina and I booked Ray for a two-day canoeing course. We met in a café in Llangollen, where we sat down for a pre-course chat over coffee. He asked about our experience. We had recently returned from a two-day circumnavigation of Anglesey, so we told him of this, which seemed to impress him. Then I casually said, 'I plan to paddle a canoe around the UK.'

I'll never forget Ray's face as he spluttered into his coffee. His eyebrows rose, and his lips began to curl into a smile as he replied sceptically, 'Oh, and when do you plan to do that then?'

Over the course of the next couple of days, while paddling with Ray, I told him of Davis's and my climbing and mountaineering exploits, and, before we headed back home to Yorkshire, he told me that he gave me a 50% chance of completing the trip.

Ray and I became friends. He was helpful, honest and full of wisdom. His endorsement was reassuring and, to an extent, legitimised our audacious plans.

Now, I said to him, 'Hi, Ray, it's Colin … We've done it. We made it through the Pentland Firth!'

Excitedly, I described our white-knuckle ride to Ray, foolishly telling him, 'That's it. The crux is done. It's in the bag now.'

Ray was impressed that we had succeeded in travelling through the Pentland Firth, but he wasn't as naive as I was.

'You've still got a long way to go yet, but I'll shift your chances of success up to 80%.'

Afterwards, it gradually dawned on me that Ray was right. I had popped the champagne cork prematurely.

12

The First Big Crossing

17th – 18th May 2017

Next to the harbour master's office in Wick is the control point for an offshore wind farm which was in the process of being constructed in the North Sea. Nautical charts covered the walls and numerous computers displayed weather forecasts and wind speeds across the sea. The people working there had been extremely helpful in giving us regular weather updates and, while standing in their company, looking at a map on the wall, Davis and I half-jokingly contemplated a 65-mile crossing of the Moray Firth from Wick to Peterhead. Those around us laughed nervously at the idea of us making a crossing like this in a canoe. As it was, at this stage in our journey, we didn't have the courage. A few weeks further along, and who knows?

A steady breeze left a manageable but lumpy sea as we left Wick surrounded by incredible, dramatic scenery. Endless cliffs dropped into the water, and hundreds of noisy seabirds filled the sky.

After a relatively easy 25 miles, we pulled into a small bay at Berriedale, hidden amongst cliffs. A calm river flowed into a lagoon and seeped out to the sea. We pitched our tent on a grass embankment in front of picturesque cottages looking out to the horizon. Thousands of squawking seagulls broke the tranquillity. As we absorbed the scenery, a man in his mid-fifties came over to us bearing welcoming cups of filter coffee. He was a cartographer who had mapped large areas of the Scottish coastline. We chatted about our journey and his job. I had previously heard of cartographers who, for fun, would write their names in the contours of maps, hidden but in clear view. We laughed together as I asked him if he was ever tempted to sign his work in this way. He denied any such thoughts, telling us that all of his work was too closely checked.

Davis and I came to the mutual decision that this was where our crossing of the Moray Firth would start. The shortest direct route from here to the Moray coast was 41 miles.

We set off at dawn, paddling into a bright, calm sea in a light breeze. This was the first time we had ventured into such an expanse of open water. Our destination was out of sight, beyond the horizon. Non-stop paddling as the wind gradually petered out was hard work, but we were excited about our first open crossing. It felt good to know that we were making progress.

20 miles in, and Davis's seat broke, probably in protest at his dynamic paddling style, and half an hour of faffing ensued. The repair kit was neatly stowed away in a barrel and thus almost inaccessible. I eventually managed to wrestle my way under the spray deck to dig it out, and was just thankful that the sea was calm – any rougher and it would have been an impossible task. Davis performed an improvised repair on the broken seat hangers using cable ties and cord, and we continued paddling, having learned a lesson about the accessibility of the repair kit.

Five miles further along, though, Davis's whole seat collapsed into a pile of wood and fabric that looked like an old set of bagpipes. It was broken beyond repair. We replaced it with a waterproof rucksack, but this was too low and slid about as Davis paddled. I could tell that he was in pain as, every few minutes, he was forced to stop paddling, stretch his spine and adjust the rucksack.

'You ok, Davis?'

Davis turned and looked at me.

'Yeah, I'm ok.'

But his face gave away his predicament. He was suffering, but there was nothing I could do.

The remaining 16 miles were uncomfortable for Davis, and I tried to end the crossing as quickly as possible by paddling harder and harnessing as much wind as we could in the sails.

We landed on a sandy beach near Findochty, where Davis set up camp while I went looking for any old bits of wood on the beach that we could use to fix the seat. In the distance was an elderly lady with shoulder-length grey hair, wearing a big coat. She was walking her dog and appeared interested in what I was doing as she walked towards the canoe. I explained what had happened and that we needed to fix the seat by morning.

Without hesitation, she said, 'Don't worry. Come to my house. My husband has lots of wood.'

I confess that I didn't relish the thought of spending hours with this lady. Deviously, I volunteered my partner. 'Hey, Davis, can you go with this lady to get some wood while I sort things out here?'

So, without much choice in the matter, Davis climbed into the lady's car and they drove away.

An hour later, he returned, pale and slightly shaken, with a nervous smile on his face. To this day he describes the journey as the scariest moment of our entire trip. The lady's driving had been perilous. She had lived in the area all her life but had turned the wrong way to go home and got lost – perhaps the effect of having a strapping young man beside her in the car.

Nonetheless, her act of kindness saved the day. Davis returned with three cut lengths of timber decking, complete with holes drilled at the end. We lashed these into the boat to create the perfect seat, and it lasted the remainder of the trip.

13
Reflecting on the Missing Link

19th May 2017

5 am saw us back on the water for the first tide of the day in a choppy sea. We paddled and sailed eastwards towards the tip of the Morayshire coast. In the distance, to my left, I could see the faded grey silhouette of the undulating Caithness coastline, which we had left the previous day. It felt surreal and almost unbelievable that we had crossed this expanse of water in such a small craft.

Our first stop was the stony beach of Downie Bay, tucked in beside Troup Head. The weather varied between sunshine and gusty showers, requiring us to take shelter under our tarp. Out at sea, a pod of dolphins swam past, their dorsal fins breaking the surface as they saluted our journey. Dolphins are guaranteed to put a smile on the face of even the weariest of canoeists.

At rest, Davis and I chatted fondly about our very first experience of the Moray Firth, when we had paddled a section of it as part of a journey which we named 'The Missing Link'.

~~~

It was 2016, less than 12 months before the big trip. After our first canoeing adventure around Skye, I had known that Davis and I had the makings of a good team. But we needed another test – one that would involve long distances, hard paddling and little sleep.

I was aware of a two-day expedition that Ray had completed several years previously. He and Chris Charlton had paddled the length of the River Spey, from Loch Insh to Spey Bay, in one day, a journey of some 60 miles. They went on to paddle the length of the Caledonian Canal the next day, another 60-mile journey from Fort William to Inverness. This sounded like a great training trip, and one I would like to complete. But what about the bit in the middle – the 60-mile stretch of coast between Spey Bay and Inverness, that would link these two journeys together?

We were at a friend's wedding, an occasion we didn't want to miss. After offering our congratulations at the reception in Fort William, we left for Loch Insh, the starting point for our adventure.

From Loch Insh, the River Spey winds past the Cairngorm mountains towards the sea. Every turn of the river provides a view worthy of hanging in a gallery. Calm waters interspersed with rapids provide a superb challenge for the canoeist. The river flows, shallow at times, over gravel beds with weeds flowing like hair in the current. The Spey is a salmon river, the presence of the fish given away by the occasional splosh as a leaping fish flops back into the water and the numerous anglers usually standing patiently in the cool waters, casting their lines and waiting for a bite. But a Sunday was a statutory day off for the fishermen.

We set off at 4 am from the eastern shore of the loch and headed into the river aboard our trusty 17' Penobscot, loaded with expedition sailing rigs, camping gear and enough food for five days. The day started cold and misty as we guided our canoe past fallen trees.

As the sun rose into a clear sky, we paddled with the gentle flow of the river. It was hot, hard work, and we soon realised that drysuits were not ideal attire. I didn't want to get wet, though, and, as this was only Davis's second venture out on moving water in an open canoe, we couldn't guarantee a dry passage.

As we landed with relief in Spey Bay, conditions had cooled down considerably. We had remained dry on the outside but were cold and wet with sweat inside the drysuits. It was 8 pm, and we had been on the go for 16 hours.

As the Spey flows into the open sea of the Moray Firth over a shingle beach, the smooth waters of the river, no longer protected by its banks, give way to swell and surf.

We climbed into our sleeping bags, tired but content. The alarm on my watch went off just three hours later. In one of those 'am I really doing this?' moments, I wriggled out of my sleeping bag into the cold. The thought of leaving the confines of the river and launching into the sea in the dark was daunting. Starting at 1 am meant that we would catch the west-flowing tide towards Inverness.

Davis and I paddled our canoe towards the sea in total darkness, and, as we did so, the swell increased along with my nervous tension. Waves could be heard breaking on the beach, their boom amplified out of all proportion. With only a hint of wind, we paddle-sailed towards the distant lights of Lossiemouth.

Cruising in shallow, sandy waters, we landed on the beach at the mouth of the River Findhorn at 8 am. The tide was now against us, and we had to wait.

Five hours later, we were back in the canoe. The sun was high, the air was windless, and it was hot. I empathised with sailors stranded in the doldrums. We kept paddling. I was concerned that if we didn't make Inverness by 7 pm, we would be against the tide. It was a neap tide that day, but the tidal flow on the approach to Inverness is strong, and I wasn't sure we would be able to paddle against it.

Sometimes, you need a bit of luck in life. With ten miles to go, the tide turned against us once more, but the wind picked up, giving us just enough momentum to paddle-sail past Fort George and towards the bridge on the A9 at Inverness.

It was 8 pm when, exhausted, we landed at the entrance to the Caledonian Canal and set up camp.

Day three saw us awake at 4 am. With 60 miles left, we used every puff of wind to help us on our way, but, as any canoeist or sailor knows, the wind is frustratingly unpredictable. For the first part of the day, along Loch Ness, there was only the slightest movement of air to help us, but, as the day progressed, we were blessed with a pleasant breeze, giving our tired muscles a chance to rest as we sailed along Loch Lochy and Loch Oich, and back into the man-made canal at Gairlochy.

Finally, almost out of gas, as the setting sun was casting a glow over Ben Nevis, we landed at the top of Neptune's Staircase in Banavie. I felt fantastic. I had a good partner, and anything was possible. Over three days, we had completed a stern 170-mile test along a river, sea and lochs. I knew then that we were a strong team.

~~~

As we reminisced, the weather improved into the second half of the day. The tide took us past the towns of Rosehearty and Fraserburgh. Within the space of 20 minutes, we had drawn alongside two other vessels – a small fishing boat and a RIB (rigid inflatable boat) with a photographer on board. The friendly skippers asked what we were doing, and, to both, Davis replied, in his understated way, 'Canoeing around the UK.' I'm not quite sure I believed it myself.

As we rounded the corner, leaving the Moray Firth behind and heading into the North Sea, the shallow water gave way to wide sandy beaches, rising into tall dunes. Mariners are warned of these treacherous, shallow waters by the impressive 120-foot high Rattray Head lighthouse. Not far from this, on a small surf, we pulled into the beach and hauled the canoe 200 metres up the soft sand, out of the sea's grasp. By this time darkness had fallen, and our next job was to find a campsite, which was no easy task in this desert of fine sand. With no choice but to pitch our tent in the shelter of a dune, we used bags and barrels to secure the guy lines. After a quick late meal of Beanfeast and pasta, we set our alarms for another early start. I climbed into my damp sleeping bag. My mind was playing tricks on me, because the tent seemed to rock as though I was still in the canoe. I fell asleep listening to the sound of the tent flapping as the wind increased in strength outside.

14

A Casualty Amongst Many

20th – 21st May 2017

The tranquillity of yesterday had vanished and a keen wind cut in from the sea. Big North Sea rollers, five deep, were breaking in lines over the length of the beach. Beyond the furthest waves, the sea looked calm enough for us to paddle, but launching our canoe through the surf would be perilous.

Like two Generals heading into battle, Davis and I studied the disheartening scene, looking for a consistent gap that we could sneak through without being overturned. It looked marginally quieter near the lighthouse, which was acting as a breakwater, so we decided to launch there.

The canoe's sails flapped in the wind, and Davis, recalling our crash landing through surf two weeks earlier, asked, 'Shall we take the sails down?'

I gave a lazy and ill-thought-out reply, 'Nah, we'll be ok.'

So began our ordeal. With Davis holding onto the front of the canoe and me at the rear, we waded in through the surf. Waves of opaque green curled and broke before us, their residual power lifting the boat and causing us to stumble.

We struggled deeper into the water as wave after wave broke around us. Looking for a gap in the relentless onslaught, I saw an opportunity.

I was up to my waist in water, and Davis was up to his chest. I jumped into the rear of the canoe, inadvertently dropping my paddle into the water. I anxiously shouted, 'Get the paddle.' Davis waded towards the shore in pursuit of my prized blade. Any hope of safe passage through the surf had gone as the next wave drove towards us like a truck.

In an instant, just as the wave was at the point of breaking, it hit the front of the canoe, flipping it high into the air in a spectacular backwards somersault. I was ejected like a rider being hurled from a horse, tumbling into the surf. Cold water filled my drysuit from the open neck as I cartwheeled through the foaming white soup.

Davis and I staggered through the surf to the canoe, which was on its side, full of water, being battered by waves. Each blow sent the stricken boat surging forward only to be sucked back by the remorseless undertow into the path of the next wave. I knew there was no way it could have survived undamaged.

We worked frantically, trying to pull the canoe clear of the sea and back towards the beach as the waves expended their last joule of energy around our feet. Apprehensively, we inspected the damage. The aluminium rigging on both sails was broken, but we were lucky, and everything else seemed ok. We had got off lightly. Rattray Head is the site of many shipwrecks, and the remains of some of these can still be seen on the beach. Thankfully, our canoe was not going to be joining them that day. Every expedition needs a bit of luck.

Soaking wet, with the din of breaking waves in our ears and the wind in our face, like surgeons in an operating theatre, we lost no time in immediately beginning to repair the damage. Both sails were unusable, but, using basic tools and rapid-setting epoxy resin, we were able to transplant parts of one sail onto the other, saving the life of our mainsail. This was enough for now. We could do further repairs later, but we needed to get going, as the tide waits for no one.

Within 45 minutes of our first attempt at launching, we were back in the canoe – this time with the masts down. Paddling like escaping convicts, we broke through the final line of waves into the flat open sea beyond, where we were able to raise our one remaining sail. I'm sure that, in his head, Davis was cursing my decision to leave the sails up, but he didn't utter a word. He didn't need to. I knew that this was my mistake, and it could have cost us the trip.

We paddle-sailed for the next few hours in complete silence. Mist covered the shore and the poor visibility added to our sombre mood. I tried to console myself by focusing on our positive response to the crisis. Yes, I had cocked up, but we had made a good recovery.

An eerie fog pervaded the air as we slipped quietly past Peterhead harbour. The shore was barely visible, and we were navigating by GPS alone. The restricted visibility brought a real danger of collision with other vessels and both Davis and I kept a nervous lookout. We continued past steep, rough, grey cliffs, noisy with seabirds, their bases white with breaking swell.

Nearing Cruden Bay, the gothic Slain Castle came into view – its presence felt appropriate in the now driving rain. As we neared the entrance to the harbour, the paddling became difficult, and the canoe hardly moved. With the tide against us and the wind causing a hindrance, what should have been a leisurely ten-minute paddle took us over an hour. Nothing was to come easily that day.

Eventually, we pulled our canoe up a small slip, and a friendly local fisherman let us take shelter in his lock-up container. We clambered out of our dripping drysuits, hung them up and, like miners after a shift at the coalface, went to the pub. Passing a souvenir shop, we impulsively purchased a bright green bucket and spade, although we had no intention of building sand castles. Instead, we planned to use the wooden handle of the spade to make further repairs to our broken sail.

It had been a long day. We set up camp on the grass beside the little harbour, and an older gentleman, a local fisherman called Pete, came to see us. We chatted with him for a while before he went home, but he returned later with tins of food. We were blown away by his kindness – the generosity of those we met along the way would be a hallmark of the whole trip.

The following day involved a difficult ten-mile journey to Aberdeen. On the approach to the busy harbour entrance, two young children were playing on the beach with their father, who was watching us intently. As our canoe slid onto the shore, we wearily stepped out onto the sand, unfolding ourselves like rusty penknives.

'Hi, I'm Michael,' the man said, holding out his hand. 'I've been following your progress on Facebook since the day you set off. It was fantastic watching you cross the bay.'

Michael presented us with a bottle of whisky and a cash donation to charity. I didn't have the heart to tell him I was teetotal and Davis didn't drink whisky. It was another special moment for us both.

15

Aberdeen to Skateraw

22ⁿᵈ – 24ᵗʰ May 2017

The small, pretty villages punctuating the rolling countryside and flat beaches we passed were giving way to busy towns and cities. The deserted waters of the north and west coasts merged into busier seas, where large cargo vessels loomed on the horizon.

We had replaced the broken mizzen sail with the spare that Katrina had been carrying on the van, and left Aberdeen for a 24-mile slog to Inverbervie. The wind, a light southeasterly, rendered sails useless, meaning that paddling was the only way forward. Calm seas are usually welcome, but, today, a stomach-churning one-and-a-half-metre swell meant that seasickness was never far away.

At our planned destination, there was no suitable harbour to land the canoe. The tide had turned, and we needed to stop for a rest. Wearily, we carried on with heavy arms to the small quiet fishing port of Gourdon. Two extra miles is a long way when the tank is empty and the body is aching. This leg of the journey had felt exhausting. My diary entry for the day summed it up:

'Paddled all the way. Got to Inverbervie. No harbour. Last two hours against the tide. Hard day!'

The following day was much the same. Davis and I were struggling. The wind and swell were on our nose and, later, to make matters worse, so was the tide. The fishermen's buoys were being sucked under by the flow, confirming our suspicions that a strong tide was running against us. Paddle-sailing, tacking and gaining little ground for a lot of effort, we doggedly made our way towards Arbroath. The spires of St Andrews hovered enticingly in the distance, but that would have to wait for another day.

Eventually, we laboured into the shelter of Arbroath harbour and pulled the boat up the narrow sandy beach surrounded by a maroon block sandstone wall. Katrina, waiting for us, had already spoken to the harbour master, who had kindly agreed to allow us to use the showers there.

The prospect of washing away the sweat and stress of a hard day on the water was very appealing. The shower block was in a small purpose-built building with a key-code entrance. Inside, hanging on the wall, was a large map of the UK.

Curiosity took me to the map to see how far we had come. This was a big mistake – my heart sank. I traced our journey from Strontian to Arbroath and was pleased with our progress until I looked at how far we still had to go. I scanned the remainder of the journey, and I felt weak. There was so much of Britain still to cover.

We had been through so many hard days already, but a colossal task still lay ahead. The vast stretch of coastline from Arbroath back to Strontian drained my confidence and left me feeling flat. I walked out of the shower block, struggling to shake off the burden of another 1,500 miles of the unknown.

I took a deep breath and faked a smile. I had been in this position before when climbing. Sometimes it is better to take one step at a time and not even consider the summit.

We spent the evening eating a big dinner with stodgy puddings in a seafront restaurant while we planned our next big crossing to Skateraw, a distance of over 40 miles. We were due some challenging winds, so prepared ourselves for another day in the North Sea battlefield.

Compared with the previous day, this day started off feeling like a breeze. The offshore wind was helpful, the sea was calm, and the tide was pushing us along. We were in good spirits. The map in the shower block was parked at the back of my mind, firmly out of the way. It was back to business.

I much prefer offshore to onshore winds, as they feel more comforting. Blowing from the land to the sea, they create smaller waves in the shelter of the land. There is a smaller chance of being swept onto rocks, but it's important to be careful to avoid being blown out to sea.

Steadily, the wind strengthened, and the bright sun reflected off a dazzling cobalt blue sea. The waves grew in size. On occasion, they slammed into the side of the boat, drenching us, as we leaned the canoe into them to counteract their force and prevent a capsize.

By now, the wind had ensured that I stopped paddling to concentrate on sailing and keeping the canoe the right way up and on course. At the same time, I was scooping buckets of water from the bottom of the boat and throwing them overboard.

As the wind increased, so did the size of the waves and my levels of anxiety. I knew that, if things were to get much worse, seeking shelter would be our only option. Our escape would be the Isle of May, a nature reserve. I steered a steady course to pass close to the island, giving us a chance of landing there if we needed to.

Gradually, the wind eased off and the waves began to break less. We were in a good mood. As concern gave way to relief, our journey again felt fun and exhilarating. Majestic gannets soared in squadrons as I sat on the gunwale sailing and bailing while Davis paddled hard.

Landing at Skateraw, we pulled into a sheltered lagoon-type sandy beach. There, we met a curious woman with two children. 'Wow, you guys looked like something from *Swallows and Amazons*.'

Another gent, Duncan Ellis, had been watching our progress on the live Spot Messenger feed and had come to the beach to say hello. Wishing us well, he presented us with a fine pot of delicious homemade beef bourguignon and a bottle of wine. This was a kind gesture, with the added bonus of relieving me of my cooking duties.

Skateraw sits beside the ominous Torness nuclear power station. As we departed the following morning, aiming to leave Scotland behind us, the unnerving alarm sounded at the power station, like something from a disaster movie. Maybe they knew something of what we were about to face.

16

Reaching England

25ᵗʰ – 28ᵗʰ May 2017

We had survived over 500 miles of hard canoeing and learned some valuable lessons. Our boat skills and understanding of the seas had improved beyond recognition. The impact of the weather and tide was now much easier to predict. We were evolving from rookies into hardened coastal canoeists.

Reaching England was important. Not because I dislike Scotland. On the contrary, I love Scotland with its wild coastline, welcoming people and freedom to camp, but England was another milestone and getting there represented a psychological boost to our morale.

As we left our beach at Skateraw, the ominous slate-grey, rectangular structure of Torness nuclear power station receded into the distance as we paddled in calm seas and sunshine. We knew that this wouldn't last, as strong onshore winds were expected.

Sure enough, we were soon bouncing through steep oncoming waves. The bow plunged into the chop and a constant spray of cold water covered the canoe. I watched as Davis occasionally threw his body to one side like a boxer dodging a punch as a wave crashed over the bow into his chest. Despite receiving steady jabs and the occasional right hook from the sea, he never missed a beat with his paddle.

Water sloshed around my ankles, adding to the flotsam of biscuits and dried fruit which had found their way into the bottom of the boat. I felt as though I was on a never-ending treadmill of paddling, adjusting sails, navigating and bailing. No matter how much water I scooped out of the canoe, it was back within minutes. I resigned myself to a hard day's graft.

My shoulders, arms and bum ached. My legs and knees pushed uncomfortably against the side of the canoe to keep it balanced. I distracted myself from the pain and toil by continually scanning the scenery and coastline, drifting into my own little world with thoughts of people and places.

Passing the cliffs of St Abbs Head was particularly rough. The easterly headwind was impeding our progress, forcing us to make unhelpful tacks into large, occasionally breaking waves. The boat lurched from crest to trough, where the waves were high enough to shelter us from the wind.

'Keep going' was my internal mantra.

Conditions were starting to ease when Eyemouth came into sight. We had a choice to make. We could put an end to our current struggle by landing and waiting for better conditions, but we would still be in Scotland. This would have felt like a failure. We planned to reach England, just ten miles away.

We stopped paddling to look around and assess our predicament. Between here and Berwick-upon-Tweed, the coast was a long, high, vertical cliff with numerous caravan parks along its edge. The cliffs dropped into shallow water where the oncoming swell broke in waves, leaving us nowhere to land. To carry on would leave us without an escape route and no choice but to make it to our destination.

With mixed feelings of determination, commitment and apprehension, Davis and I agreed that we should keep going. One concern was that, should we be seen by someone from one of the caravan parks, they would think we were in difficulty and ring the coastguard. I carefully monitored my VHF radio. Thankfully, no alarm was raised.

Eventually, the high walls of Berwick-upon-Tweed harbour came into view, jutting out to sea at right angles to surf-swept sandy beaches. Thankfully, we reached the safety of the shallow, sand-choked harbour and paddled in to land on a steep golden beach. We were in England, having survived 22 miles of tempestuous seas.

As we hauled our canoe onto its trolley and pulled it to safety, a yacht, the occupants of which had decided to take shelter from the wild seas, followed us around the harbour wall and ran aground. Helpless, we watched with admiration as, with cunning use of the engine and a bit of careful manoeuvring, the skipper was able to free the wallowing vessel.

Camping here was awkward and would have meant leaving the canoe unattended. The beach, as a result of the sunny weather, was becoming busier with people. Strong headwinds forecast for the next few days forced a much-needed rest on us, and we decided to spend our time in the van with Katrina.

We had just finished eating our now staple diet of junk food when a van pulled up alongside us in the carpark.

Looking out of the window, Katrina said, 'It looks like we've got a visitor.'

Davis slid the van door open to reveal a bearded, athletic-looking, middle-aged man wearing a beanie hat – this was Oliver Jay. Ollie was a charismatic canoe and kayak guide whose expertise was on the east coast. He oozed knowledge of the area's history, geology and wildlife. More importantly, he was able to give us advice about the tides around the Farne Islands, which lay just a few miles to the south.

The next morning, I decided that it was time to give the canoe a check over. As I peered inside the hull, I couldn't believe what I saw. I was starting to wear a hole through the bottom of the canoe. There was a deep gouge, caused by my constant scraping of the bailing bucket as I evicted tonnes of water from around my feet. I brought out the repair kit. Armed with foot lengths of Keel Easy tape and a camping stove, I glued a repair in place, thankfully preventing further damage.

Davis and Ollie joined me. They had returned with Ollie's camcorder to interview us. Davis in particular did not like media attention – it just wasn't his thing. Davis is a quiet, thoughtful guy who doesn't like to boast of his achievements, and this adventure was a personal challenge for him. But Ollie put us both at ease as he asked us about our journey so far. The result was a relaxed, light-hearted interview.

Later that day, as we were resting in the van, we were hit by a dramatic thunderstorm. I lay on the bed as lightning lit the sky and cracks of thunder shook the van. A cold sweat came over me as I started to imagine what I would have done if we had been at sea in this storm. My answer was that we would have tied ourselves in, taken the sails down and paddled as hard as possible to the nearest shore. From this point, I viewed every dark nimbus cloud with intense suspicion.

~~~

Thankfully, two long days of enforced rest saw us back at sea. Our departure was an unbelievable contrast to our landing. Gone was the wild wind and breaking surf, and the sea was calm and beguiling. Both wind and tide were on our side. We made good speed past the tidal island of Lindisfarne, its simple, low-lying appearance disguising its importance in history as an early home to Christianity and the scene of bloodthirsty, merciless Viking raids. We passed magnificent Bamburgh

Castle, on the site of the original ancient seat of the kings of Northumbria.

On reaching the Farne Islands, Ollie, who was there with a group of sea kayakers, greeted us. I smiled to myself as I saw the familiar signs of disbelief on the faces of the kayakers at the sight of an open canoe, sporting two sails, heading around the coast. Stopping briefly to chat, we said our goodbyes and continued on our journey. Passing the coastal town of Seahouses, we were joined by a pod of bottlenose dolphins. They accompanied us for five minutes before disappearing. It felt good to be on the road again.

17

The Yorkshire Coast

28ᵗʰ – 31ˢᵗ May 2017

We paddled past long sandy beaches and arrived at the small natural harbour at Boulmer, one of the last remaining fishing villages on the Northumberland coast. This sanctuary is formed by an almost complete circle of rock with a small gap where boats can gain access to the sheltered safe waters – a gift from nature to small boat owners. As the tide rises, the water fills the harbour through the gap, creating a strong flow. When the tide falls, the water rushes out of the gap, back to the waiting sea.

After a night in the tent beside a thin strip of beach, we rose to find the incoming tide pouring into the harbour. This was our only way out, and we both had doubts about our ability to paddle against such a stream. Deciding to give it a go, we paddled frantically up a discernible step of fast-flowing water. After a hard, synchronised paddle, we were out into the sea, heading south towards Blyth.

A dull and showery day with light winds made for an easy passage as we pulled passed Blyth's steep 18ᵗʰ-century harbour walls onto an uninviting sandy beach. This was a busy harbour with both working and pleasure craft of all shapes and sizes coming and going. I felt like a trespasser.

Too lazy to cook, I took a walk into town for fish and chips, only to find that I had turned the wrong way altogether. A long walk later, I located the busiest chippy I had ever visited. There were rows of serving hatches, each with a queue of people, like the stalls at a football match. Orders were taken by a cashier using a microphone headset. My order was sent back to the fryer and, seconds later, I was handed two huge portions of fish and chips. This was a chippy on an industrial scale, a long way from the family-run, two-person chip shop I was used to. It's no wonder our fish stocks are dwindling and our bellies expanding. We ate the fish out of long cardboard boxes under our tarp, filled our flasks, and left on the evening tide for Sunderland.

The wind was in our favour and, paddle-sailing, we made good progress. Our concern was the mist, which had become heavy and a serious hazard to shipping. With our eyes and ears peeled, paddling like a pair of meerkats on high alert, we kept as close to shore as possible and were cautious around the walled harbour entrance of the Tyne, illuminated by faint flashing lights.

Wild camping was becoming difficult, and we had arranged to meet Katrina again. Neither of us fancied sleeping rough in Sunderland, and the van was a welcome sight as we pulled into the shelter of the vast harbour walls.

We awoke with a sense of optimism. It was going to be a good day, and, with luck, we would be in Yorkshire by teatime.

For almost 30 years, Yorkshire had been my adopted home. People tell me I have developed a Yorkshire accent and I do have a liking for flat caps and Yorkshire Tea. I was looking forward to paddling here, along a coast that I had seen many times from the shore but only once from the sea.

Our next stop was a sunny, groin-lined beach at Redcar. From here, a much more pleasing coastline unfolded. Clifftops and green fields are punctuated by small fishing villages. Neatly painted houses in contrasting shades of green, pastel blue and yellows tumble into valleys that run to the shore. I mused on the tremendous seas these villages must have been witness to over the years – a far cry from the situation as we paddled through the calm waters to Whitby.

Whitby is a fascinating town – busy, yet peace and quiet are never far away, and colourful, noisy and friendly with a history stranger than fiction. With links to the Romans and Vikings, and home to the imposing Whitby Abbey, Dracula, Captain Cook, whale and herring fishing, Whitby Jet and, of course, fish and chips, Whitby has it all.

I could see that Davis was impressed as, in the rocking boat, he laid his paddle down and took out his camera to photograph the Gothic abbey, which stands aloof on the cliff above the town. The sea was now confused, with clapotis as waves rebounded off the harbour walls. The canoe lurched like a spent rodeo bull as we neared the harbour.

As we paddled through the tiny harbour entrance, the water calmed and we entered another world. Ahead was the River Esk and, on either side, the seaside town. Tourists eating chips and ice cream watched with bemused interest as we paddled up the river. This was a welcoming place. Katrina had spoken to the harbour master, who couldn't do enough to help and allowed us to moor the canoe on a pontoon and use the showers.

Ahead of us lay Flamborough Head. This massive intrusion into the sea obstructs the flow of billions of tonnes of tidal water, creating a boiling sea that lurked in my imagination like an ogre. Katrina and I had paddled here several years before. We had been forced to retreat as the seas grew to a size that neither of us had previously experienced, threatening to sink us. With the mental state of a boxer going into round two after taking a first-round beating, I was stepping into the ring once more.

After a restless night, I awoke at 6 am to a cool and dewy morning. The town was empty and still. The calm of the River Esk and Whitby was soon behind us as we paddle-sailed along the coast.

Helped by the tide, we cruised passed the Yorkshire village of Robin Hood's Bay and the vast surf-washed bay of Scarborough. Filey Brigg came into view – a thin spit of land with continual 20-metre cliffs providing a long natural breakwater which guards fine golden beaches. As we reached its point, I became very nervous as we were confronted by a line of tall breaking waves over a natural limestone reef, blocking our approach to the beach. Any attempt to land here would be foolhardy. Only when Davis realised that we could paddle behind the reef did I relax. My misapprehension left me feeling a bit silly as we paddled past swimming holiday-makers onto the beach.

We knew that our next leg would test us. Dismissing my nerves, Davis and I pulled the canoe up Filey's curving beach. The bay sweeps along the shoreline and gives way to six miles of steep white limestone cliffs, culminating in Flamborough Head.

18

Flamborough Head

31st May – 1st June 2017

The members of Filey Sailing Club were amiable, making us tea and giving us somewhere to hang out while we waited for the tide to turn. I was keen to glean as much local knowledge about the waters around Flamborough Head as possible. I knew that the next 17 miles to Bridlington Sailing Club would be hard.

The wind from the east was increasing, stronger than forecast and blowing straight into our faces. Small white caps decorated the sea as we said goodbye to our hosts. Pulling the boat across the long stretch of flat wet sand, we arrived at the water line and launched into small surf waves. After a brief paddle into deeper water, I raised the sails, forcing us into a tack directly towards the daunting cliffs before us. It was clear from the offset that making headway was going to be a struggle. We consoled ourselves that, once around the headland, the same wind would blow us to Bridlington.

The wind heeled the canoe erratically, making sailing and paddling difficult. This was aggravated by the fact that we were taking on a lot of water and consequently needed to do a lot of bailing. I watched landmarks on the cliffs, but they hardly moved. Our slow progress was disheartening to say the least.

The seas started to rise as the strength of the easterly wind continued to increase. The swell rose and fell like the chest of a giant sleeping bear. For a few seconds, we had a windy 360-degree vista, then we fell into a surround of water. The waves were wildly erratic in a way I have never seen before, and some span like mini tornados.

We planned to reach Bridlington on the other side of the head. If the going was too hard, the old lifeboat station at North Landing, near the tip of the head, could offer us refuge. Our last resort was to return to the beckoning bay at Filey.

Reflecting on the battle Davis and I found ourselves in the midst of, I realise that I was suffering from summit fever, as the condition is known in the mountaineering world. Our determination to make progress over-ruled level-headed decision making. We had been fighting a headwind and big seas for over four hours when North Landing came into view. The small beach and lifeboat slip lay, hazy, at the foot of the sea-washed cliffs. With our energy and resolve almost spent, it would have been sensible to stop here, but we didn't, choosing instead to fight on.

Time was running out. The tide soon turned against us, making the dash to Bridlington excruciatingly hard. To make matters even worse, in a couple of hours, darkness would fall. I don't know what Davis was thinking. Communication was difficult over the din of the wind and the noise of the sea breaking against the cliffs. We continued our cycle of frantically paddling, sailing and bailing our swamped canoe in the extreme conditions. By now, turning back was unthinkable.

Slow, laborious progress was made by hugging the cliff line and paddling without the use of sails. Alert to the prospect of being swept onto rocks, we could see that we were moving, creeping in the right direction. Our doggedness left us with only a mile and a half to go before rounding the head. The sun was setting.

Very gradually, the cliffs gave way, and we turned the corner. It was an immense relief to see the distant lights of Bridlington and to finally have the helping hand of the wind. All that now remained was a paddle-sail, in darkness and against the tide, to Bridlington Sailing Club where we would camp for the night.

To make ourselves visible, we donned bright headtorches as we located the sailing club which, according to our map, was at the harbour. Paddling past a small group of lairy, jeering commercial fishermen at the harbour entrance, we landed on a pontoon, cold, wet and totally spent.

I found the deputy harbour master and explained what we were doing. We learned that the sailing club was just a building in the town centre and the club proper, where we should have been, was further down the coast. Neither of us could face getting back in the canoe, so I negotiated for us to leave our boat at the harbour.

The deputy contacted the harbour master on the phone, who berated us for not asking his permission to land. I apologised for our mistake, and he became sympathetic, allowing us to leave our boat there for the night. It was past 11 pm, and, with nowhere to camp, we decided to get a taxi to the proper sailing club with our essentials and collect the canoe in the morning.

I looked at Davis, who was pale and drawn. He had put everything he had into the last 18 miles, and I suspect I was in a similar state. The relief of getting around Flamborough Head was incredible, but the adrenaline that had driven us was now dispersing, and I suddenly felt exhausted.

'Davis, I think we should have a day off tomorrow.'

He nodded in agreement.

It was into the early hours before we got to sleep in our tent. Our alarm was set for 7 am, which would allow us time to get back to the harbour and collect our canoe. We planned to paddle the two miles to Bridlington Sailing Club and then go for a cooked breakfast.

In the morning, a gentle stroll beside the beach on a bright, calm, sunny day, past multi-coloured chalets, took us to the fishy-smelling harbour. We donned our buoyancy aids, climbed into the canoe, and paddled along the coast to our tent at the sailing club. This was the shortest leg of the trip.

Our decision to take a day off was a good one. We had a visit from our friend John Gilbert from the Pennine Canoe Club. He and his daughters took us out for lunch at a cafe. It felt strange to be drinking a frothy coffee in the sunshine when, just 12 hours earlier, we had been fighting for survival. Both Davis and I were relaxed, the stress of negotiating Flamborough Head gone, and we enjoyed the company.

Later in the day, my sister, Davis's Mum, joined us. Full of beans, Kate, three years older than me, has lived a wild life filled with great joy and tragedy. Now living in southern Ireland with her husband Sean, she has found her vocation caring for the elderly. Kate's visit was good for us. Her matter-of-fact appreciation of life and loud laugh could only serve to make us smile.

19

Lincolnshire and The Wash

2ⁿᵈ – 8ᵗʰ June 2017

An easy 25 miles along brown, mud-stained waters, clear evidence that the sea was eating into the coast, took us to the seaside town of Withernsea. Landing through steep, dumping waves, we hauled the canoe up a slipway that ran into the busy promenade. The town was bustling with holiday-makers, and this was clearly not the right place to leave our canoe and equipment. A bivvy or camping hereabouts would have exposed us to the mischief of youth.

Our priority was the boat. Davis stayed to look after it while I went for a wander, looking for safe storage. I came across a council yard which housed a fishing boat on a trailer. Looking like Max Wall in my skin-tight black leggings, I walked into a group of fishermen surrounded by creels, sitting on makeshift chairs and passing the time of day.

A young, tough-looking chap covered in tattoos, wearing a tight T-shirt and rigger boots, greeted me in a loud voice, 'Fuckin 'ell it's Rudolf Nureyev!'

Everyone burst out laughing. I had become quite used to wearing tight black leggings under my drysuit but had forgotten that they made my legs look like two skinny black carrots.

Beneath their rough exterior, these were good people. Their laughter turned to intrigue as I explained what Davis and I were doing and talked about our journey so far. They were more than happy to help, and offered us the use of their yard as a secure location to leave our canoe for the night.

I spent some time talking to one of the fishermen. He was a similar age to me and been fishing since he was a child. He had seen the rise and fall of the industry. I asked him if he had ever considered another career.

'I'll never do anything else. I'm not interested in money, and I don't want a nine to five job. Fishing is in my blood.'

Our conversation turned to crossing the Humber estuary, an area where he had worked all his life. His advice was priceless:

'Speak to the coastguard and tell them what you're doing. They'll tell you when it's safe to cross the shipping lanes.' As a throwaway comment, he added, 'And keep away from the tide race at Stony Binks.'

Now that the boat was safely secured, the next thing Davis and I had to do was find a campsite. A taxi took us to a commercial monstrosity that, thankfully, didn't have room for our tiny tent. Eventually, we found a small family-run campsite which was perfect for us.

~~~

When we were planning the trip, I imagined that the east coast of England would be boring, with miles of dull, flat coastline, mediocre beaches and nothing to break the horizon other than busy seaside towns and industrial harbours. In many ways, I was right – it's certainly not as scenic as, say, the west coast of Scotland, but there was a charm to it. To my amazement, I found myself enjoying this part of the journey.

To get away from the monotony of paddling, my mind was engaged continuously – the ancient formation of the shallow sea, the Romans, the Vikings, industrialisation and the fishing industry all captivated my imagination. I found the flatness inspiring and the views sometimes unimpeded and vast. The beaches varied in colour and texture. Some appeared like ribbons of multi-shaded sand and pebbles, striking a subtle contrast to the vast sky. I pondered the possibility of paddling to the European continent, just a few hundred miles across the North Sea.

Crossing the Humber estuary was one of the most fantastic canoeing days I have experienced. The paddling was easy, close to the shore and through a teal green flat sea. We were heading towards Spurn Point, a land formation as remarkable as any mountain. This long, flat, worm-like peninsula extends from the mainland for three miles, isolated at the mouth of the Humber estuary. Made of minerals eroded from further up the coast, it is a unique habitat, home to birds and wildlife and now a designated nature reserve. Just off Spurn Point, submerged rocks at Stony Binks threw waves to the surface where they broke, creating a magnificent white contrast to the surrounding waters. The sky was bright and unbroken, and the whole scene was unforgettable as we continued along, pushed by a strong tide. The currents manifested themselves in whirlpools and riffles of white water.

As advised, I had made contact with the coastguard, who granted us permission to cross the busy shipping lanes of the estuary. Davis and I laughed as the operator put out a general warning to ships on the distant horizon:

'To all ships approaching the Humber estuary, there is a very small, I repeat, very small, vessel crossing from north to south. Please be vigilant and slow down. Thank you.'

We couldn't believe that these huge ships were being told to slow down for us.

The crossing was easy, but dithering in a shipping lane is like tying your shoelaces in the middle of a motorway, so, working hard with our paddles, we moved at an excellent 5 mph, and, steadily, the southern side of the estuary came clearly into view.

In front of us, I saw some big red circles on the beach. 'Hey, Davis, that looks like a target … for aircraft… oh shit!'

It dawned on me that we had strayed into a bombing range. Checking the map, we were close to Donna Nook, an RAF range. There was no patrol boat keeping vessels clear. Reluctant to disclose my lack of planning, I made contact with the coastguard and confirmed that there was no firing taking place that day.

The beautiful, warm, golden beaches hereabouts were lined with hundreds of grey seals sunbathing as others escorted us through the shallow waters towards our next stop near Chapel St Leonards. It was like a scene from a David Attenborough documentary, and I felt privileged to see such a wildlife spectacle.

Our peaceful wild campsite near Chapel St Leonards on the north Lincolnshire coast was tucked away in a grassy clearing behind the dunes. I felt relaxed and happy after a great day as I watched a cuckoo flying across lush meadows. Sleep came easily in my stress-free state. The weather forecast was perfect for our next open crossing, The Wash.

I had become acutely aware of the sea and how its appearance changed around our coastline. It had been a deep, dark blue in the north, where the water was much colder. The warmer southern waters, paler in colour, seemed friendlier and less potent than those exposed to the massive fetch of the Atlantic – perhaps an illusion.

From Cleveland southwards, erosion of the coastline was evident. In parts, churning waters were stained chestnut brown as millions of tonnes of earth was scraped off low, soft cliffs and dissolved in the sea. Remnants of farm buildings, once standing proud in the fields, had collapsed on the shoreline, awaiting their watery fate. Others, abandoned, perched precariously, waiting for the sea to claim them.

Crossing The Wash was an easy day spent paddle-sailing past endless wind farms. Everything was in our favour, with a steady north wind and helpful tide. Our destination was Wells-next-the-Sea, where the only difficulty was finding the channel between sandbars which would allow our passage into the inland waterway. Eventually, we found it, and a two-mile paddle past small moored boats of all shapes and design took us to the sailing club in the bustling Norfolk seaside town. We secured the canoe and walked along the busy waterfront, where children and adults alike were parading buckets of recently caught crabs. We sat outside, enjoying the sunshine and eating fish and chips.

At 4 am the following day, a paddle upstream was needed to ensure that we caught the south-going tide. Out in the open, difficult navigation across sandbanks saw us cruising towards the day's objective – Happisburgh (pronounced Haysborough).

I relaxed in the canoe. We joked and laughed as we slid past seals asleep in the sea, their heads sticking up above the water, eyes closed, whiskers like guitar strings, oblivious to our presence. Cromer Pier came and went, then the wind changed direction, and things got hard.

What followed was one of those paddles where there was no enjoyment, fear or worry. It was just painfully hard. Neither of us considered stopping short, and our labour eventually brought us to the breakwaters at Happisburgh. Relieved, we landed on the beach in front of the lifeboat station, where Katrina had made arrangements for us to leave the canoe in a secure yard.

For the next three days, a storm was due to lash the east of the UK, and Norfolk would be subjected to gale-force winds.

Continuing our journey was out of the question, and we were forced to take a few days off.

Katrina and I have friends near Norwich, Kelly and Andy, who we had met through racing kayaks in Nottingham. They own Broadland Paddlesports, on the banks of the River Yare, and they invited us to park our van outside their clubhouse for a few days while we sat out the storm.

The stop was a fantastic break that both Davis and I needed. At the clubhouse, Andy cooked hearty evening meals for us. By this time, Davis's appetite, like his paddling, was voracious. After a big meal, which would fill most people, he would merrily devour an entire cheesecake as though it was the normal thing to do. Both Katrina and I had acclimatised to Davis and his cheesecake Olympics, but I'm not sure our hosts had seen anything quite like it.

After three days, the storm passed and the forecast was for much lighter winds. Rested and refuelled, we were keen to get back into the canoe.

20

The Thames Estuary

9th – 12th June 2017

Slowly and perceptibly, the next hazardous section of the journey was creeping up. I was learning that, in deep waters, with less friction from the seabed, waves are likely to be smaller than those in shallow water, which is prone to big waves developing. Like the swell coming into a beach, the waves build and break only when the water is shallow enough to slow its base so that the crest continues its forward momentum before toppling over. For this reason, the shallow North Sea has a reputation for rough conditions.

We were nearing Suffolk and ahead lay the extremely shallow waters of the Thames estuary. To the uninitiated, this area looks easy to negotiate. It doesn't carry the notoriety of the Pentland Firth or Portland Bill (an area we were yet to become acquainted with). Its position between Suffolk and Kent provides a degree of shelter. Tidal flows are moderate, and there are no spectacular stomach-churning tide races. But, in its benignity, danger lurks. Shallow water pushed by the wind and tide forms a big breaking sea, and the many sandbars are hard to navigate and have potential to leave a canoeist in untenable waters. Navigation is complicated, and if, as for us, the plan is to cross directly from Suffolk to the Kent coast, there is nowhere to hide.

From the shore, we followed a small tributary of the River Alde inland to a tiny tidal pool at Orford Haven. The banks were made up of thick, dark grey, smelly mud, of the consistency of grease. The tide needed to be high for there to be enough water to float the canoe and for us to escape back to the sea.

It was a beautiful windswept spot. A raised shingle beach protected the marshland from the sea, and the area was home to avocets, harriers and egrets. For two days it was also to be our home.

Our plan was bold and involved cutting straight across the 47 miles of the Thames estuary to the Kent coast. We would thus avoid the difficulties of going inland and, if successful, would cut down our journey by at least a day.

Katrina contacted one of the sailing clubs on the Kent coast in the hope that they would be able to provide us with somewhere to leave our canoe.

We laughed as the Commodore refused our request: 'I'm sorry, we won't be able to help. And besides, the waters around here are not suitable for a canoe!'

The yacht club at Margate was more helpful, and so we decided to head there.

The weather gave us just one day of opportunity, but the forecast wasn't inspiring, with strong southwesterly offshore winds. Some decisions are easy but others sit on a knife edge. Whether or not to cross the Thames estuary on this day was one of the latter.

The F5 to F6 winds were at the limit of what we could deal with and from a direction that meant they were just enough not to be a headwind, but things would be close. Get it right, and we would be on the verge of turning another corner, but a wrong decision could mean the end of the trip or worse.

I was heavily influenced by the fact that we had a one-day window which, if we missed it, would leave us stuck for several more days. Fortune favours the brave. After a sleepless night and a lot of deliberation, we decided to leave at 7.30 am and head out to sea. If we felt uncomfortable after ten miles, we would turn about and head for land near Felixstowe.

A cold, blustery start saw us bouncing through waves past shingle spits, heading into the most demanding 12 hours of my canoeing career. The sails were at 45 degrees to the wind, not generating as much power as we had hoped. We dug in, paddling hard. The hazy visibility and cool winds added to the serious feel of the day.

After ten miles, Felixstowe came into view to our right, and we reached our cut-off point. I shouted to Davis over the noise of the wind and sea, 'What do you think, Davis? Keep going?'

Davis thought for a mere second before responding, in such a way as to suggest I had asked something ridiculous, 'Yeah, keep going.'

We were managing well on a bumpy ride through a confused sea when, suddenly, I could see lines of white crests as waves broke in front of us. They were of a size that presented a real danger to our canoe. I steered a course away from them, but more soon appeared. We were left with no choice but to step into the arena.

We were in the thick of battle. In my mind was a haze of thoughts: *'keep paddling, we're filling up, bail, bail, that one's gonna break, hold on, paddle.'* The boat was unstable and water sloshed around my seat. I knew things were bad when Davis stopped paddling and began to bail.

In the troughs, we were surrounded by waves taller than our mast. I don't think either of us was scared because there simply wasn't time. Our only way out was to keep going.

I found myself in my own world. While bailing, I leaned into the bottom of the canoe, scooped buckets of water and, in one motion, emptied the contents over the side. The sides of the canoe provided shelter, like the walls of a trench. For a second at a time, there was an escape where I enjoyed a momentary peace away from the unceasing turmoil.

We passed a wind farm, and, gradually, the wind eased to an acceptable level and the sea became manageable. The Kent coast was visible for the first time, and I steered a course as we paddle-sailed towards Margate.

With five miles to go, Davis shouted, 'We're not going to make Margate, we're against the tide.'

Unbelieving at first, I soon realised that he was right. Using an anchored ship as a transit, it was clear that we were stationary. Our lack of progress wasn't helped by the wind, which was now in our faces.

We changed course by just a few degrees, enough to get us out of a stalemate, and headed further east to Joss Bay.

After what seemed like hours, Katrina met us as we stumbled out of the canoe, utterly relieved that the ordeal was over. 'How did it go?' she asked.

Davis's reply summed it up. '12 hours of the Pentland Firth, but worse!'

As we sat in the van, eating and planning for the next day, it was hard to believe that we had spent the day fighting for survival through the biggest seas I have ever been in. Maybe the Commodore at the first sailing club we had contacted was right.

21

White Cliffs

13th – 16th June 2017

We needed an easy day, and we got one. A glorious 17-mile stretch of milky blue, calm waters and a gentle breeze for assistance took us to the stunning chalk cliffs of St Margaret's Bay.

Katrina had launched a drone and was busy filming us paddling our way to the shore. Tyke and Gonzo knew I was coming so, excitedly, they ran onto the beach to greet us.

What a bizarre situation we found ourselves in as we landed. Katrina was being issued a fixed penalty ticket for allowing the dogs on the beach. Despite our charitable cause and epic endeavour, the warden was immovable.

A local fireman, Shaun, had been swimming in the bay and saw us land. Intrigued, he came and spoke to us. A friendly, helpful chap, he was the perfect antidote to the warden. He invited us back to his home for a meal, which we readily accepted. He gave directions to his house, where we agreed to see him later in the evening. This left us time to have a wander up to the white cliffs.

I have spent a lot of time hanging off all sorts of cliffs, from small 15-foot-high boulders to 3,000-metre-high walls on El Capitan in Yosemite and many others in between. Here, though, I was taken aback by the bright white, flint-peppered, vertical chalk cliffs which dropped sheer into the English Channel. As I walked along in the sunshine, I got close to the edge. I noticed that, in places, the grass near the edge was patchy and almost dead, although I didn't think anything of it.

That evening, as we ate our meal and chatted effortlessly with our hosts about our walk to the top of the cliffs, Shaun explained, 'Yeah, those bits of dead grass are a death trap. The grass dies through lack of water due to erosion of the cliff below. A few people have fallen to their deaths because of this.'

~~~

Our spirits were high, another corner had been turned, and we were heading west along the Kent coast. Our next obstacle was the Port of Dover, the busiest ferry terminal in the world, catering for over 13 million passengers and 300,000 tonnes of freight each year.

Paddling under the white cliffs towards the harbour, I contacted the VTS coastguard, which controls safety in this area. They were extremely helpful and arranged for an escort boat to meet us at the eastern entrance. Sure enough, a small working boat pulled alongside and bobbed around next to us. The captain came out of the cabin and shouted to us, 'Stay there and wait for our signal, lads. When we start moving, you start moving and follow us. We're just waiting for a big 'un to come through.'

We waited in a wavy sea for a couple of minutes and then, with a low hum, a large passenger ferry began to emerge, its bulbous bow ploughing through the water as it began its journey to France. It was an awesome sight. Once it was clear away, the escort boat set off, and we followed through the churning waters on our way.

We approached the vast, steep, pebbly beaches of the Dungeness headland through a small but entertaining tidal race. Once through this, we noticed another working boat speeding towards us before spinning alongside the canoe. We turned into the wind and stopped. The stern-looking skipper came on deck holding up a large card displaying a VHF radio channel. I had the same sinking feeling that comes from being pulled over by the police. I turned my radio to the requested channel, not knowing what we had done wrong.

The skipper, friendly enough, announced, 'You can't go any further unless you want a big detour. The range at Lydd is operating 'til 5 pm and there's an exclusion zone all around it.'

Relieved, I replied, 'No problem, we'll stop on the beach.' I had always fancied visiting Dungeness.

With a few hours to kill, we spent our time dozing, sunbathing and exploring. As we lay on the flint pebbles, a shabby-looking fox staggered past from breakwater to breakwater, like a rabid dog in the desert, scrounging for food from the many fishermen.

~~~

Hastings was busy as we made our way past the pier. Davis laughed as I recounted a story from my youth involving copious amounts of alcohol, when, fully clothed, thinking it would be a laugh and egged on by friends, I had jumped off this pier in the dark, not knowing whether the tide was in or out … I was lucky.

After a shaky landing, past a chalky outcrop threatening to damage the canoe, we realised that there was nowhere to store the boat. As darkness had fallen, we paddled to a section of beach close to the main road where Katrina had parked. We slept in the van with one eye on the canoe.

A restless night on a busy road with holiday revellers and a 4 am start was always going to leave me weary, but, once in the boat, our cruise along the coast was sublime. Conditions were quiet as the swell swept under the canoe. We paddled close to shore, the silence broken only by the sound of pebbles being washed in the easy sea. A glimmer of lights in the distance betrayed the coastal resort of Eastbourne. The sky was clear with stars slowly fading, promising a beautiful sunny day ahead.

We passed Pevensey, the beach where, in 1066, the Norman invaders landed and changed the course of history. Then, after a long effort, we approached Eastbourne. Its white seafront hotels had been in our sights from the start of the day but never seemed to get closer as we paddled along the wide bay.

The clear, pale blue sky seemed to fuse with the white cliffs. Swooping vertically to their boulder-strewn bases, the cliffs merged into a turquoise sea. A small red and white lighthouse warned ships of the dangerous shallow waters. This was Beachy Head, the highest chalk sea cliff in Britain at 531 feet, its name an adaptation of the French name Beau Chef, meaning beautiful headland. It was, indeed the most beautiful headland we had ever seen.

Along the coast, the white cliffs of the Seven Sisters descended into the wide bay of Cuckmere Haven. This was our stop for the day. Here, the River Cuckmere flows from the land to a flint pebbled beach before running briskly into the sea. Floating the canoe along the river offered a welcome labour-saving opportunity and a change from our usual long carry of boat and equipment up a steep beach.

Taking advantage of this, we tracked our canoe upstream. Tracking is a traditional canoeing technique involving two long ropes tied to the bow and stern of the canoe. Pulling on these enables us to control the angle of the canoe. This means that the boat can be pulled easily against the flow without being pushed to the side. It was satisfying to be able to use a traditional skill on our journey. As the river deepened and the flow slowed, we were able to paddle further inland along the river to a sheltered spot below a pub carpark, where we moored the canoe.

The following day, deceived by the still, sheltered water of the river, we launched out into the sea against a stiff headwind. From the start, it was hard graft, with big waves against us. Mutually, we made the decision to go back and wait for a more favourable wind. The investment of effort wasn't worth the return. Had this been earlier in the trip, we would have slogged it out.

22

The South Coast

17ᵗʰ – 23ʳᵈ June 2017

The south coast wasn't my cup of tea. It was busy, with beaches full of holiday-makers, and every sort of craft you could think of milling around in the water – sit-on-top kayaks, paddleboards, speedboats and annoying jet skis. The water from Selsey Bill into the Solent brought a multitude of tankers, naval ships and ferries.

Up to this point in my canoeing career, my experience of big ships had been limited to the occasional Caledonian Macbrayne ferry and fishing boats on the west coast of Scotland. In these waters, I just kept my distance and knew that they were not to be messed with.

Our average paddling speed was 4 mph but a ship can easily travel at 25 mph and, in the case of the Seacat passenger ferry in the Solent, can reach a whopping 39 mph. A cargo vessel can take up to five miles to stop, and if, by some miracle, they spot an impediment in their path, the chances of them altering course are slim. Changing direction could mean their leaving a shipping lane, and the waters on either side might not be deep enough. The lives of the crew as well as the ship and its cargo would all be at risk.

Big ships are remarkably quiet. Often, their engines could only be heard at close quarters – a low, ominous drumming. We never knew if a boat was sneaking up from behind, and we regularly looked around, like canoeing owls, to ensure that we weren't about to be run over.

Despite our vigilance, it wasn't always easy to work out a vessel's path. A big ship ploughing in the direction of the canoe might appear initially as a matchbox-sized shape on the horizon, which would gradually grow bigger and bigger, inducing increasing panic. The ships churn relentlessly through the sea, unstoppable, leaving you not knowing which way to go to keep out of their path.

Davis and I developed a strategy for any sighting of a big ship: stop, watch, establish its course and decide whether to turn about, wait for it to pass, or keep going. Methods we used to determine a ship's course, if we were not sure from merely looking, included the use of land-based transits and compass bearings.

There was no wind, and paddling was a hard, relentless slog in a waveless, busy sea once we passed Selsey Bill. We were glad to land on a warm shallow beach on the Isle of Wight.

By this time, we had been on the go for 46 days. We were a fast, efficient team, both fit and paddling well. If the weather was fair, we made good progress. Our knowledge of the sea had improved beyond recognition along with our understanding of our own abilities. However, the honeymoon period of our partnership had also ended and, inevitably, we had some disagreements.

When we were under stress, small issues that would, in normal circumstances, be inconsequential and easily dealt with, became magnified, blown up out of all proportion and minor things, too petty to even remember, irritated and gnawed. To compound matters, I spent hours each day in silence, looking at the back of Davis's head with no indication as to what he was thinking. This lack of eye contact made communication difficult. I do not doubt that Davis found some of my actions equally annoying. I guess neither of us wanted to upset the other, and things were left unsaid – we just carried on, with our frustrations unaired and festering.

This was the way of things when Davis didn't help as I struggled to light the petrol stove on the beach. I didn't ask for his help. Instead, I struggled on, in my head thinking, 'Why isn't he offering to help? Can't he see I'm struggling? He should be offering to help, the bastard!'

Looking back now, I feel foolish. I'm sure that, had I said, 'Here, Davis, give us a hand', he would have been happy to help, but at the time I was furious, and my stubbornness prevented me from asking for assistance. As the daily stress of canoeing at sea built up, where bad decisions could have catastrophic consequences, my tolerance was wearing thin.

Following my internal tantrum over the stove, we paddled the evening tide in silence to the beautiful Thorness Bay. My irrational anger dissipated like fog in the sun, and we bivvied without shelter, watching a beautiful sunset. The next day, we left the Solent behind us.

Another magnificent day was dawning as we paddled quickly past Hurst Castle, which protected the entrance to the Solent. The tide flowing through a constriction picked up at this point, and a few easy waves broke up the calm seas as we headed towards Christchurch.

We met Katrina and headed to a beach café for respite as we waited for the next tide. We were chatting easily, drinking coffee and eating cake, when I noticed a small, beautiful, pale green cricket sunbathing on the wall next to us. 'Hey, Davis, Kat, look at this', I called.

Captivated by this elegant, perfectly formed insect, we sat and watched. Then, like an arrow out of nowhere, a starling boldly swooped past us. In one swift movement, this speckled assassin landed on the wall, picked the cricket off with its beak and flew away. In an instant, the beautiful cricket was gone. We sat in gloomy, stunned silence. You never know what's around the corner.

The second tide of the day took us neatly to Swanage, flanked by limestone sea cliffs. Memories of my early climbing days came flooding back. I remembered being an inexperienced, 15-year-old schoolboy, 100 feet above a whispering sea on a blindingly hot summer day, climbing into a no-man's-land of vertical white limestone. My last piece of protection, placed with a trembling hand, had fallen out. Ropes were now useless, and a fall would almost certainly be terminal. My arms were weak, and I was too scared to take a hand off the rock to wipe away the stinging sweat that ran into my eyes. With my face pressed against the rockface, I muttered obscenities to my legs, urging them to stop trembling. I knew that I had to do something. To try and climb down would have meant a certain fall. My only escape was upwards, into the unknown. Through a bone-dry mouth, I prayed to God, swearing that I would never climb again and always be good if He let me escape from this vertical nightmare.

I was completely absorbed in this moment of fear. A mental shove borne out of a survival instinct broke me from the chains of paralysis, and I shuddered upwards. Every sketchy move was as precarious as the last, each threatening oblivion. The world around me fell silent, as though even the sea and seagulls were holding their breath, as I reached the sanctuary of the clifftop.

Later that same afternoon, I was climbing and praying again.

~~~

The harbour at Portland is intimidatingly massive. It has a fascinating history, as old as England, from the time of the Romans to the present day. During the Second World War, it was subject to 48 air attacks. In 1940, Stuka dive bombers sank HMS Foylebank here with the loss of 176 lives. Today, the harbour is a civil and commercial enterprise and plays host to a range of recreational sailing and diving.

We approached the southern entrance, which seemed the most obvious. As we neared, I contacted the harbour master who, helpful enough, directed us to the middle entrance, one-and-a-half miles away – a long way when you're shattered after a 22-mile, hot, tiring paddle. We asked permission to enter by the southern entrance. After conferring with the Royal Navy, which had several ships moored in the area, permission was granted, but we were advised to watch out for a sunken ship at the entrance.

As we began our paddle in, Davis shouted, 'What's that?' He pointed to a black, almost ruler-like thing flapping on the surface of the water five metres away. It was obviously attached to something living. I turned the boat for a better look and saw the oddest creature I have ever seen in the sea, a sunfish. It was ungainly, with a flat circular body, two feet in diameter, and wallowed on the surface like a broken toy, flapping around for a few seconds before disappearing.

~~~

Portland Bill is an almost triangular, rocky island sticking out into the English Channel and attached to the mainland of Dorset via a spectacularly thin isthmus of shingle beach. Just off the point, where the water is shallow and the seabed rocky, east- and west-going tidal streams collide, resulting in massive, dangerous tide races.

Timing our passage around this point was essential. After careful planning, we set off. We aimed to stay within 100 metres of the shore, where deeper waters enabled a smoother passage.

As we paddled through the harbour and into the sea, about six other yachts had the same idea. It was heartening to know our plans concurred. Seeing these vessels, I was reminded of my Dad, who, during conversations about canoeing, would jokingly say, 'Colin, when are you going to get a proper boat?'

An apprehensive, adrenaline-fuelled, five-mile paddle-sail took us past the point. Conditions were calm, and there were no signs of major disturbance on the sea. Katrina filmed us as we passed the red and white lighthouse before waving goodbye to us from the shore. We laughed as I took a video of Katrina taking a video of us.

We were relieved. A weight lifted from our shoulders as another obstacle now lay behind us without drama. Others were not so lucky, as Katrina witnessed:

'An hour after watching Colin and Davis round the point of Portland Bill, I took Tyke and Gonzo for a walk along a beautiful coastal path. From here, I could see the tide race, which they had managed to avoid, developing. I couldn't believe it when I saw a yacht under motor with its bow sending sheets of water all around as it crashed through waves. What a difference an hour makes.'

The remainder of the day was bright and sunny, with a perfect breeze. A fast paddle-sail past the golden curving expanse of Chesil Beach took us to the mouth of the River Axe at Seaton. The flow of water from the river was considerable and too strong to paddle against. We landed on the beach and pulled the canoe onto the sheltered bank. This was a charming place where we could relax after our day's work. Davis and I stepped back in time and, like a pair of kids, went looking for snakes. We didn't find any snakes, but a few beautiful slow worms made our day.

12 miles was all the distance we could manage the next day. After a launch down steep pebbles, we laboured into a headwind that ensured we would work hard for any progress made. We pulled into another sublime bay at Budleigh Salterton. We paddled through the mouth of the enchanting River Otter. Trout broke the surface as we made our way upstream, leaving the canoe on the side of the river.

About 500 metres away, Katrina had parked the van in a large carpark overlooking the river. We could see our canoe and equipment, which pleased me as the beach was busy and I was nervous that someone would tamper with it.

As we relaxed in the sunshine, I let my eyes drift down the river. I couldn't believe it. A man was beside our canoe, rummaging through one of our blue barrels.

I jumped up, shouting, 'Hey, Davis, he's going through our stuff!'

Davis looked, and his face darkened as he quickly agreed with my assessment. In an instant we were off, storming along the riverside path towards our boat. Davis raced past me, knees high, fists pumping, and took the lead. With 100 metres to go before impact with the suspect, I realised that the man was, in fact, an innocent fisherman, bent down near our canoe, rummaging through his own blue box of fishing gear.

With seconds to go before Davis would surely bulldoze the man into the river, I shouted, 'DAVIS! STOP!'

To my supreme relief, Davis also recognised our mistake and skidded to a halt. Breathless, we burst out laughing. The fisherman had no idea what was happening and will never know how close he was to becoming a casualty at the hands of two men trying to canoe around Britain.

Another weather forecast of strong headwinds the next day made for an enjoyable day off and a barbeque on the beach. Our next stop was to be Brixham, 19 miles away.

23

Capsize

24th – 25th June 2017

The busy tourist and fishing harbour of Brixham is an ideal haven for boats and was the perfect place for us to stop. Multi-coloured, pretty houses line the area above the port, alongside a multitude of hotels and restaurants. It is the quintessential Devonshire seaside town.

A slipway offered an ideal exit from the water, and a helpful sailing club provided a secure compound for the canoe. Content with the 19 miles we had covered that day, the tides and our energy levels dictated that we spend the night where we were, and leave the following day.

The pressures of the journey were continuing to build. Petty issues that had already been grating on my nerves were growing. That morning, Davis and I had been getting ready to leave when we realised that we could no longer tell our waterproof jackets apart as the names which had been written on the inside had worn off. Passing him a marker pen, I had asked him to re-write his name on his jacket, which he did … in big, bold letters across the front of the hood, visible to all. I was fuming.

It was an expensive jacket which Katrina and I had paid for, and he had soiled it with no consideration for its value. I felt that this was continuing evidence of Davis's lack of regard for the equipment which was essential for our journey and needed to be looked after. After a brief angry exchange, I walked away, fearing that I would say something I might regret.

As Katrina and I walked the dogs that evening, I ranted to her about my escalating feelings of frustration towards Davis.

'I've had enough. We've put five years' worth of effort and a lot of money into this trip and I don't get any thanks, just negativity. He's got no respect for the kit, and I'm not putting up with it. When we get back to the van, I'm going to tell him.'

'Tell him what?'

'To go home. I'll finish the trip by myself.'

'Please don't, Colin.' Katrina was upset and pleaded with me, 'At the rate you're going you'll be home in three weeks. You can put up with it for that amount of time, surely?'

I agreed to sleep on it, and see how I felt in the morning. Looking back, this is an excellent example of how minor things on any expedition when people are under stress can be blown out of all proportion. I was so lucky that Katrina was there as a rudder, keeping me on track. Davis, on the other hand, didn't have a proper sounding board for any mounting resentment he needed to air. I realise now that Davis must have felt very alone at this point. It is to all our credit that we moved on, our focus on the task ahead. There is no way that I would have been able to finish the journey without Davis.

Leaving the harbour was easy. Our sheltered approach to Berry Head was on smooth waters. From there, we followed a rugged coastline with rocky islands, bays and cliffs. Initially, the going was easy, but, gradually, the winds rose to a gusty F6. Our comfortable day was turning into a challenge. The strong winds caused the numerous yachts to heel well over, even with heavily reefed sails, as they bounced through the surf.

To make progress, it was necessary to sail, but, with the strong headwind, tacking was essential. Sailing was precarious, as the whipping gusts could easily capsize us. I sat on the gunwale, leaning back to counterbalance the lean of the canoe. I allowed the sheet controlling the sail to slip through my hand when a strong gust came. In addition, I bailed buckets of water back into the sea as Davis paddled, putting his all into helping the sail to gain forward momentum.

The wind was blowing against the flow of the tide, making for big, steep waves running towards us. As the front of the canoe went over these, Davis was left hanging in mid-air. The boat would then drop down with a smack, splashing into a deep trough, soaking Davis and filling the canoe. Each wave had the effect of a brake, frustrating our efforts.

Many days had gone by since we had last worn drysuits. The weather on the south coast had been warm, and we were confident in our ability to keep dry. Dry trousers with a long-sleeved top under our buoyancy aids were now the norm. If the weather became cold, we would stop and put on waterproof jackets or more clothing. While this kept us comfortable, it would not keep us dry if we fell in. At this point, there was no time to reflect on our choice of attire, as we fought along the coast towards Dartmouth. We were in the middle of a melee.

A point came when it all became too much. As we recovered from each big gust, another would hit, then a big wave, then another gust. The canoe rocked violently from side to side, and Davis and I lurched backwards and forwards, trying to compensate for the wind, fighting to keep the boat upright. Suddenly, I felt my composure vanish, and I knew that a capsize was inevitable.

One mile before the entrance to the River Dart, frequent gusts were taking their toll. The seas were becoming untenable. Finally, we were hit by one gust too many. We toppled in slow motion into the sea. The cold water took my breath away. It felt like the Devil's tongue on my back.

Without any need for direction, our response was instant. We swam to opposite sides of the canoe. Taking hold of the leeboard, Davis slowly pulled the boat upright, the sails noisily flapping in the wind. In one swift movement, he crawled into the canoe and began expelling the water. I held the boat steady with one hand and tried to bail water with the other. I shouted to Davis that I was coming in. He moved his bodyweight to the opposite side of the canoe to counter my weight as I kicked my legs and pulled myself out of the water. We continued to bail, and, when enough water had been cleared, I removed the mainsail and replaced it with the smaller mizzen.

It felt good to be so slick, moving with the swiftness of a Formula One pitstop team. Rapid bailing helped to warm us up and donning waterproof tops kept the wind off. Only a few minutes passed before we were on the move again but, like other retreating yachts around us, we changed course and headed for the shelter of Dartmouth harbour.

In calmer conditions, we paddled gently down the mouth of the River Dart, the feet of our dry trousers sloshing with water. We cruised easily past the turrets of the 14th-century castle into the harbour. Dartmouth was another stunning Devonshire port.

Far from being shaken by our capsize, we were happy with how we had dealt with it; but for that day we had been through enough and were happy to stop.

24

The Final Corner

26th June – 2nd July

26th June – 2nd July

Through blistering heat and windless, still waters we ploughed the canoe 33 miles to Wembury, with its small sandy beach, café and tiny sailing club.

The bay is overlooked by the Great Mewstone, a sloping island lying in the sea half a mile from the beach – windswept, rocky and deserted. It had not always been uninhabited – in the 18th century, a gentleman found guilty of a minor crime was punished to seven years of exile on the island. He eventually made it his family home, which says a lot for life in 18th-century Devon. The War Office subsequently bought the island as it was in the firing line of Wembury Point Gunnery School (I assume that the family had moved out by then). The upside of the island being in the line of fire is that people kept away and wildlife thrived. Today, the island is a nature reserve.

On leaving Wembury, we paddled past the Mewstone and the mighty naval harbour of Plymouth came into view. Various naval ships, including a huge aircraft carrier, were on the move, signalling by flashlight to one another in Morse code. Jets could be heard but not seen as they blasted through the skies. A naval exercise was clearly ongoing. I often wonder what they thought when they saw us as we paddled along their flanks in waters not usually frequented by canoes. I was glad I hadn't elected to buy a green boat, or I'm sure we would have been intercepted as spies or special forces. The weather was deteriorating, and the grey sky offered a fitting camouflage to the naval ships.

Our landing that day was at Pentewan, a small beach, the majority of which is private. We left our canoe discreetly at the edge.

Sleeping that night was difficult. It rained heavily, and my body ached. Some big days now lay behind us, and I was tired.

The following morning, we had a cream tea in a local café and headed back to the van to plan the day's passage. Katrina and I pored over the maps and tidal atlases. Juggling poor weather and winds with tidal streams and a place to land was not easy. We formed a plan which I then proposed to Davis, who was also tired and feeling the strain of the last few days. He casually looked up from reading, with his feet up on the sofa, to dismiss my plan: 'It won't work.' He immediately looked back down at his Kindle.

My tiredness and frustration boiled over. 'I do all this work, and you just sit back and criticise! I wouldn't mind if you had a plan!'

To Davis's credit, he didn't say anything in return, and I immediately felt bad for losing my cool. Katrina was obviously uncomfortable and kept quiet. No further discussion took place and, in the rainy silence, we got ready, marched to the canoe and began paddling.

I knew that I had to leave behind my bad feelings towards Davis, or they would jeopardise the whole trip. Over the course of the next 31 miles, we both gave in and shared small talk. It was clear we were both uncomfortable and wanted to end our conflict.

Midway along our leg, miles offshore, we caught up with a 30-foot yacht going our way. We came alongside the vessel, surfed its bow wave and laughed as we overtook at a speed of 5 mph, saying 'Hi' to the disbelieving skipper. Despite our fractious start, it was turning out to be a good day.

Six miles from the Lizard Peninsula, a rainy squall hit us from the west and stopped us in our tracks. In an instant, we went from making such good progress that it seemed we would be able to get around the Lizard to being brought to an abrupt halt. Steep waves rose around us and we shipped on water. Going into the wind was out of the question, so we were forced to tack. Any chance of meaningful progress and any plans to round the Lizard were scuppered. We needed a place to land quickly and found the small Cornish surf beach of Kennack Sands.

With gale-force winds ruling out any chance of paddling, this was to be our home for the next two days. This wasn't such a bad thing. Davis and I both needed a rest, so we read books, walked the dogs and relaxed. With rest came the opportunity to inspect the Lizard Peninsula. We drove to Lizard and walked across windy pastures to the clifftops, where, worriedly, we watched surfers enjoying opaque green curling waves which would cripple us in our canoe.

The staff at the Kennack Sands Surf School were extremely helpful, keeping an eye on our canoe and giving advice on local sea conditions. As the protection of the English Channel is lost and the Atlantic Ocean flows unchecked, we knew the swell would grow bigger and the seas become more serious, but we felt confident that, with a good forecast, rounding the peninsula would be easy enough.

The tides dictated a 3 pm start. The beach at Kennack was busy with tourists – curious, friendly and questioning. Watched by a group of scantily clad holiday-makers, we felt like astronauts in space suits as we launched through easy surf and headed towards the peninsula.

The wind was enough to create waves which, combined with the swell, made for a testing sea, the intensity of which was magnified when we passed the Lizard headland. The waves rebounded off the rocks and flowed back out to collide with incoming waves, and the resulting clapotis caused a problematic confusion of water. This was no place to linger. The noise of crashing waves, the wind and birds combined with the imposing dark cliffs to hurry us along.

With the Lizard behind us, our next objective was the small Cornish fishing village of Mousehole. Neither the wind nor tide were helpful. The next 17 miles were a depressing slog. Nothing came easily, and the canoe hardly moved in the water, despite our best efforts.

Our progress was pitiful and slow as we paddled into the darkness. The lit silhouettes of ships moored in Penzance seemed stationary. The black outline of St Michael's Mount, a static monument to our lack of progress, was ever-present. We pushed on and, very slowly, the lights of Mousehole harbour entrance came into view.

We landed, relieved and tired, but still on a mission to be ready for the next hurdle. It was 11 pm, and we intended to be up at 4 am to catch the tide around Land's End.

The sun rose in the sky behind us in a blaze of orange. I kept looking back, mesmerised, as we paddled towards the south western tip of the UK mainland. Despite yesterday's slog, our morale was high and we were excited to be ticking off the final corner of the UK.

I love the Cornish coast. For many years, I brought my daughters and my sister's children to Cornwall during the summer holidays for the Climbers' Club Family Meet. We used to stay at the Count House, an old house which had once been used to count the wages of the tin miners but has now been converted into a bunkhouse for climbers. On these holidays, I split my time between the beautiful sandy beaches and climbing on sea-washed, golden granite cliffs. Davis and I reminisced about these glorious summer holidays as the canoe sailed smoothly past the spectacular Minack Theatre, where we had been privileged to witness open-air performances of operas and plays with the Atlantic Ocean as a backdrop.

As we approached the south west corner of the UK, the swell rose steadily. There was more significant movement, and the waves seemed to carry more energy. They had marched thousands of miles across the Atlantic Ocean and had gathered momentum and size along the way. The sea felt more serious – agitated and stomach-churning. Paddling through these waters, I felt an undercurrent of nervousness, a feeling I had also experienced on the north coast of Scotland.

The canoe rolled and lurched remorselessly. Davis retched into his bailing bucket and threw the contents overboard. For a few strokes, I found myself plunging my paddle into coffee-stained vomit, which didn't help my suppressed seasickness, but we could see Longships Lighthouse and Land's End, cheering us in a miserable sea.

Gradually, more predictable currents, flowing in a uniform direction, flattened the sea, and our morale improved. Prominent old tin mines, a legacy of industrial Cornwall, sat isolated above the orange granite cliffs. We tried to pick out areas where we had previously climbed – not an easy task as the land looks so different from the sea. We cruised past small fishing boats and RIBs loaded with tourists looking for wildlife as we headed towards St Ives.

Entering St Ives Bay, we paddled gently past numerous bathers and paddle boarders to a slip, where Katrina met us. The contrast of the empty sea to the crowded town was almost overpowering. The town was too busy – a guaranteed headache on a hot day.

We secured the canoe in a sailing club compound. A Cornish pasty was the obvious choice for tea before we headed off to the quiet of the Count House. From here, we walked down to the sea cliffs of Bosigran and looked out over the gently curving horizon. It was odd to think that, only a few hours earlier, we had paddled past these cliffs.

The south coast of England had been testing for Davis and me. It had also, though, taken its toll on Katrina:

'I was glad to see the back of the south coast. It had been a difficult few weeks. The original plan, which involved me meeting them every five days to re-supply, had fallen into disarray. With no easy wild camping options, Colin and Davis wanted to sleep in the van each night. That was all well and good, but it created a whole load of stress for me.

First, having them in the van meant I had to feed them. I had to make regular trips to shops and supermarkets as there was only a limited amount of storage space in the van. Colin and Davis were both losing weight because of the amount of exercise they were doing in the canoe. The seals on Davis's drysuit were no longer watertight as his wrists were becoming so thin. They wanted full-fat stodgy food, so I filled the van's small fridge with things like pizza and sausages, cheesecakes and fruit pies. But I wasn't going to start cooking two different lots of food each day, so as they continued to lose weight I was gradually piling on the pounds.

Second, the van constantly needed to be topped up with fresh water for drinking and showers. Almost every day I had to find a source of water. I went to cafes, pubs, visitor centres, petrol stations, anywhere likely to have an outside tap. I told them what I was doing and asked for water.

Colin and Davis would clamber into the van after a hard day on the sea and ask,

"What's for tea, Katrina?"

"Nothing until you've had a shower."

The Thames Estuary   *photo Colin Skeath*

The "Beaucheif" Beachy Head   *photo Colin Skeath*

Tracking the canoe up the river Cuckmere   *photo Davis Gould-Duff*

Calm Seas leaving the Isle of Wight   *photo Davis Gould-Duff*

Paddling in the still waters of The Solent
photo Colin Skeath

Launching from shingle beaches, Seaton *photo Katrina Skeath*

Sunrise leaving Mousehole to go around Lands End *photo Davis Gould-Duff*

Approaching Bude *photo Katrina Skeath*

Heading towards big surf and holiday makers at Bude *photo Katrina Skeath*

West Angle Bay

photo Colin Skeath

Colin and Davis with Bill and Sue Taylor

photo Katrina Skeath

The charismatic Luke McNair

photo Davis Gould-Duff

Katrina with Gonzo watching Colin and Davis launch into the Menai Straits

photo Paul Airey

Grim faced paddlers, Donaghadee, N Ireland *photo Jude Todd*

Island of Dana, Sound of Jura *photo Davis Gould-Duff*

'They both stank!

In between shopping, begging for water and walking the dogs, I also had to find somewhere every few days to wash Colin and Davis's sweaty clothes. I'd never been to a laundrette before – I didn't know they still existed – but there I was, sitting on a small bench, waiting for the drums to stop spinning while watching the orange dots of the Spot Messenger gradually make their way across the screen of my phone.

I didn't have time to use the dryers, as I had to work out where the boys were going to land, and, more importantly, where I could park with easy access to the coast. Most carparks along the south coast have height restriction barriers, making it impossible for me to enter in the van. The carparks that I could get into all had, "No overnight parking" signs. Where possible, I would contact a local sailing club to ask permission to stay in their grounds overnight, but I often found myself parking at the side of the main road or up a small side street, hanging the boys' freshly washed clothes all over the van to dry.

The only respite for me was when Colin and Davis planned to stop on the Isle of Wight. They launched early from Littlehampton, where we had spent the night at the sailing club, and I looked on the map for a place to see them pass and take some photos. I set off driving. It was a Sunday morning, the sun was already high in the sky, and it promised to be a blisteringly hot day. It seemed that everyone in the UK had decided to go to the seaside that day. Traffic crawled along, and I was getting nowhere fast. I was tired and hot. I suddenly thought to myself, "What on earth are you doing?"

This was the first day in weeks that I didn't need to be somewhere to meet the boys, and here I was, driving along in the blistering heat, trying to see them. For what? Another photo the same as so many others I had already taken?

I saw a sign for a parking and picnic site and turned in. A deserted flat grassy parking area surrounded by woods and with *a few picnic benches was the ideal place for me to stop, walk the dogs and spend the day relaxing. I would see the boys again tomorrow.*

Now that the south coast had come to an end and Wales was lying in wait, I could relax a little and take some time to enjoy where I was. After all, the UK really is a beautiful island.'

25

Heading North

3ʳᵈ – 4ᵗʰ July 2017

We capsized as we left St Ives. We had made an early start and paddled away from a beach, which, after yesterday's bustle, was pleasantly quiet. A good breeze was blowing, and I had just raised the sails when, for some reason I'm unsure of, I was distracted as a strong gust of wind hit, taking us by surprise.

It was an awful feeling – in an instant, the boat started to tip over. We both threw our weight to the opposite side of the canoe and fought against the inevitable. It was too little, too late, and we were in the water. More by good luck than judgement, we were wearing drysuits, so we didn't get wet. Within 30 seconds of capsizing, we had clambered back in and were bailing water, the canoe moving forward again.

I looked to the shore to see if anyone had observed our mishap. The beach was deserted, and I breathed a sigh of relief. Just then, though, my VHF radio burst into life with a message from the coastguard saying they had received a call from a concerned citizen that a canoe had capsized, and asking if we were ok. Feeling embarrassed, I sheepishly replied, 'All's good, thank you.'

Over the next 32 miles, two miles offshore, we passed rocky headlands flanked by wide beaches peppered with ant-like people. The going was easy enough, but, in places, thought and care were needed as shallow waters funnelled between islands and created large swells. We turned in past Trevose Head, where a powerful tide ran against us, causing us to surf standing waves as we covered the last half a mile to shore. Here, we waited for Katrina, who offers this account of her day:

'This was probably the most stressful day of the entire trip for me. The Spot Messenger had stopped working. Once Colin and Davis set off, I had no idea where they were or where they were going to land. More importantly, they no longer had access to an SOS button, which would send an accurate GPS location in case of an emergency. I had to get the Spot working.

I tried to call the company in America, but the line just kept ringing out. Frustrated, I sent an angrily worded e-mail to their customer services department. Hours passed and I continued to dial the number. Eventually, I got through.

I spoke to a young-sounding lady who, obviously reading from a checklist in front of her, said, "You need to put new batteries in."

"They were new three days ago, they're fine."

"Well, maybe it's too cold, it won't work if it's cold."

"It's 26 degrees Celsius. Trust me, it's not too cold." We were getting nowhere near identifying the problem, and my stress levels were rising ... along with my phone bill on this long-distance call.

"I think you're going to need a new device," I was eventually told, and she offered me a small discount off next year's subscription for the inconvenience.

I started searching the internet. Where on Earth was I going to get a new Spot at such short notice? It wasn't like I could order one online and get next day delivery to my van. I made a phone call to a chandlery in Plymouth – they could get one in, but not for a couple of days. I made another phone call to another chandlery, and this time they gave me details of their suppliers. I might be able to get one directly from them. Another phone call:

"I'm supporting a couple of guys who are canoeing around the UK. Their Spot Messenger has stopped working, and I'm desperately in need of a new one. Today, if possible."

"Around the UK? In a canoe? Wow, that's some feat ... Hang on a moment, I'll see if we've got any in stock."

I crossed my fingers, hoping I would be in luck.

"Yep, we've got one here. You can have it at trade price. Are you coming straight over for it?"

"It'll take me an hour and a half to get there. I'm setting off now. Thank you so much." It was already 3 pm, and I was going to reach Plymouth around rush hour.

As I gratefully collected the new Spot Messenger, I received a phone call from a very apologetic lady in America who had picked up my e-mail. She couldn't have been more helpful in transferring our contract onto the new device. All I had to do now was to drive back to Cornwall and find my husband and nephew. This had been one of those days when I thought it would have been easier to be in the canoe.'

~~~

The following day of paddling went without incident and saw us land at Bude, a Cornish surf beach. It was my turn to be stuck with a broken seat – one of the steel bolts holding my seat together had sheared, with potential to lead to a serious problem if it were to collapse as Davis's had done almost seven weeks earlier.

On the beach, leaning over the side of the canoe, I was considering ways to fix the problem when a local gent came and offered help.

'I've got some threaded bar in my van. Hang on a moment, I'll see if it's the right size.'

I kept my fingers crossed as he headed off to his vehicle.

'Sorry,' he said as he returned to the canoe, 'looks like it's all too big. But I've definitely got some at home. I'll come back after I've had my tea.'

Sure enough, as promised, he returned later that evening and fixed my seat.

Acts of generosity and kindness like this had been commonplace on our journey, including gifts of food, drink, water and places to camp or for Katrina to park the van. We even received a freshly baked cake – our experience was far removed from the picture often painted in the media of a selfish and insular society.

26

Farewell to England

It was late morning and our departure time to catch the tide was upon us. The beach was busy and surfers were enjoying the waves. I watched them tumbling onto the beach in the surf. A knot of dread formed in my stomach and adrenaline started to flow. Flashbacks of our near disaster at Rattray Head filled my mind. I was fearful that we would be smashed as we launched the canoe. Added to this was a real risk to swimmers should things go badly, as a canoe filled with a tonne or more of water being tossed about could be lethal.

A lifeguard patrols Bude beach and I thought it prudent to ask advice about launching. I walked across the sand and spoke with a helpful, bronzed lifeguard who would look equally at home in *Baywatch*. He pointed to an area where the waves break early because of a sandbar.

'Paddle in front of this,' he said with authority. 'Wait for a gap in the incoming waves and then head out as fast as you can.'

Our canoe was at the left-hand side of the beach where a small stream runs up to an inland canal. While I was tempted to take the lifeguard's advice, it would have meant taking our canoe into the area where most of the people in the sea were. Instead, we kept to the left side of the beach, waited for a gap, and paddled for all we were worth. It was an anti-climax – not even half a breaking wave to make the fuss worthwhile. Safely at sea, we aimed the canoe towards the island of Lundy, 25 miles away in the Bristol Channel, and paddled.

Lundy is spectacular. It rises out of the sea like a giant green flat-topped iceberg. Its shore is guarded by orange and golden granite cliffs and its clear blue waters are a marine conservation area. The mainland plateau provides unbroken views of the North Devon and Pembrokeshire coastlines, which seem a world away.

At three miles long and just over half a mile wide, the island is owned by the National Trust and is home to a small population of 28. There is a tiny harbour, a campsite, a runway for small aircraft and a pub, The Marisco, named after William de Marisco, who was implicated in a conspiracy to murder Henry III in 1235.

It is a remarkable place with a fascinating history. The earliest known human occupation dates back to the Neolithic age. For such a small place, Lundy has been in the thick of it: Romans, Vikings, Knights Templar, civil war, piracy and two world wars all have a stake in its history. It has also been the scene of countless shipwrecks and two German Heinkel bombers crashed there. Now, it is a place where two fools landed their canoe during a circumnavigation of the UK. Despite all of this historical turmoil, Lundy is a quiet, beautiful retreat.

On reaching the island, Davis and I felt weak from paddling. The day had been baking hot, with little wind to help us, and we now faced a very steep path to the campsite. Oh joy …

Davis and I abandoned the canoe on the beach while we carried our camping equipment, food and water up onto the plateau to the small campsite. We sweated past The Marisco where a group of able-looking men was sitting outside.

Swinging a 60-litre barrel off my shoulders to rest, I greeted them with a 'Hi'.

One of the group, realising that we had just landed, said, 'If I'd have known, we'd have given you a hand and brought your bags up!'

I wasn't sure at first if he was being sarcastic, but we later learned that they carried the bags of most visitors to the island. I felt very unlucky – the help would have been very much appreciated.

For me, Lundy was a magical place, one that I would like to re-visit in less stressful circumstances and with more time to explore.

Across the sea to the north of Lundy lay the sandy beaches and sheer limestone cliffs of the Pembrokeshire coast. This area is home to multiple hazards, strong tides, big surf and military firing ranges.

The next day saw us crossing the Bristol Channel to South Wales. The cross tides and northwesterly wind made it difficult to keep on course. It was a constant struggle against wind and waves to avoid being pushed towards Port Eynon. Had we landed there, another day of paddling would have been necessary to get back on track. As we paddle-sailed tight into the wind, the canoe heeled over and we both hung over the gunwales. This was the nature of our long day.

Midway into our crossing, several deep, thunderous crumps of exploding ordnance could be heard in the distance from the Castlemartin ranges. This gave us something to ponder, as we knew that we would need to get past this hazard the following day.

After hours in the canoe, the welcoming sight of the sandy beach at Lydstep came into view, and we set a course for its sanctuary. The excitement of finally setting foot on dry land vanished as we realised that this was a private beach and there was no prospect of camping. Frustrated is an understatement for our feelings at that moment. We needed to find somewhere else to spend the night. Darkness had fallen as we paddled another two miles to a wonderful deserted beach on Caldey Island.

After completing our usual tidal and weather forecast checks, we slept under our tarp in what felt like a plague of jumping sand shrimps. We were glad to have left England behind.

27

Fog and Linney Head

7th – 8th July 2017

The following day presented two major hazards. Fortunately, one cancelled the other out. Our course along the coast would take us past the firing ranges at Castlemartin. We were expecting a long detour around the danger zone, but, as it turned out, the lingering fog did us a favour. After a quick phone call to the range control and coastguard, we established that firing for the day had been cancelled.

The fog was thick. Visibility down to 20 metres would usually have grounded us, especially in a busy area, but we had a cunning plan. We would hug the coastline, staying in the shallow water where bigger boats wouldn't go. As there was little wind, the risk of being caught in the swell and swept onto rocks was greatly reduced.

With this plan, we set off paddling. Following the GPS, we tried to stay within a few hundred metres of the shore. It was wonderful paddling: the perfect antidote to the slog of the previous day. With our sails redundant and the tide in our favour, we paddled easily, the silence only broken by the quiet 'shhh' of the water as it swirled around the cliffs to our right.

By mid-morning, the mist had lifted and our speed had dropped off. The tide, contradicting our information, was against us. I recalled the words of a small boat skipper who had said, 'It would be good if mother nature read the tidal charts.'

Although we were paddling hard, we gradually slowed to a pathetic 1 mph. If we stopped for just a moment, we drifted backwards.

Realising that we were probably in a tidal eddy, we considered our options. We could go further out to sea to get into the main tidal flow or get even closer to the land and try to catch an eddy within the eddy. Going further out looked daunting, so we moved closer to the shore. The swell had increased and, as we paddled only metres away from the base of the cliff, we faced the constant threat of being pushed onto rocks. We crept forward, putting a tremendous amount of effort into each stroke. I don't know if we made the right decision, but it was clear that the Pembrokeshire tides were powerful and difficult to read. Nowhere was this more evident than at Linney Head, just a short distance away.

~~~

Our hard work paid off, and, by way of reward, a favourable wind picked up, pushing us towards Linney Head, en route to the mouth of Milford Haven.

Ahead, we could see that the waters were turbulent, with tell-tale steep white-crested race waves being kicked up. Neither of us was concerned – at this point in our journey, this was just one more race. I felt like an airline pilot: 'Just a bit of turbulence – nothing to worry about.'

Confidently, we paddled head first into the egg box of waves, both paddling hard as the rodeo ride began. Gradually, it dawned on us that, even with the wind filling our sails, we weren't moving.

We paddled harder. Progress was slow, but we seemed to have escaped the worst. Then I heard the dumping crash of waves behind us getting louder and louder. I turned to see the race getting more ferocious. We were being swept back into the path of steep, six-foot-high, collapsing waves.

My confidence vanished, immediately replaced by my usual mantra of fear. 'Paddle, Davis! Paddle!'

I don't know if it was my trembling voice or Davis's appreciation of the situation, but it was like we were hitting the accelerator pedal. We pulled ourselves out of harm's way. The seething mass behind us was like a tethered, snarling Rottweiler, unable to trap us in its foaming jaws.

For the next five miles, our sails were filled with a steady wind. We were both paddling hard, and yet we could only reach a speed of 3 mph as we laboured into West Angle Bay.

After securing our canoe and climbing out of our sweat-soaked clothing, I walked into the village to look for a shop. I saw two elderly ladies talking over their front garden hedge and called to them:

'Excuse me, can you tell me where the local shop is, please?'

'I'm sorry,' one of them replied, 'we don't have one anymore. It closed last year. The nearest shop is nine miles away. If you're lucky, the pub might have some bread and milk behind the bar.'

They went on to tell me how difficult life was without easy access to a shop to buy basic provisions. I thought about the post office and small shops in my village of Strontian and the vital role they played as a focal point in the community. I felt sorry for the residents of this small Welsh village. An 18-mile round trip would have been too much. I didn't bother going any further.

West Angle Bay was fascinating. Overlooked by the turreted, Napoleonic fort on Thorne Island in the entrance to Milford

Haven, the small eroding cliff under which we bivvied had been worn away to reveal skeletons from a 9th-century burial ground. Maybe they belonged to locals who had lost their shop and starved to death. From our makeshift camp, we contemplated the heavy shipping coming and going from the port of Milford Haven, which lay less than a mile from Angle Bay.

The following morning, a small café above the beach provided us with a large cooked breakfast. Our feelings of nervous tension were rising – before us lay two notorious stretches of water between islands, causing dangerous and violent seas. These were Jack Sound and Ramsey Sound. We were checking our tidal information when Davis noticed anomalies between the charts and tidal atlases, leading him to suggest a later start to give us the easiest and safest passage. We agreed on this – our ambitious hope was to get through these two major tide races and arrive at Fishguard, some 39 miles away, without rest.

28

Jack, Ramsey and Bill

8th – 11th July 2017

Passing a fascinating ancient harbour hewn out of the rock, we left West Angle beach. Our first hazard was an unstoppable cargo ship coming our way. We drifted, eating biscuits and drinking coffee, while we waited for it to churn past us. We then continued the seven miles to Jack Sound, the narrow gap between the mainland and the Island of Skomer. This rocky channel is a natural funnel for tidal streams, where incredibly strong currents and big waves are found.

We paddled against the flow, with cliffs and rocks all around. The boiling water pushed the boat in so many different directions, giving us a sense of insecurity. Our timing was perfect, and we were happy to leave the sound behind us and push on to our next hazard, The Bitches, an aptly named tide race within Ramsey Sound.

With no assistance from the wind, we entered the sound, our senses on high alert in anticipation of the confusion that would surely follow. Gradually, our speed picked up as we paddled quickly through. I checked my GPS – while our speed appeared normal, we were flying. Pushed by the current, we were travelling at over 10 mph. Small, erratic waves danced as if they felt our excitement as we glided effortlessly though. It was exhilarating to know that the plan to leave later was working and we would soon be out of harm's way.

Our smooth ride through both sounds could have been an entirely different story had our timing been wrong or if any wind had blown.

The current continued to give us a superb push as we passed Whitesands Bay on the tip of St Davids Head. I told Davis of my trips here as a schoolboy with the outdoor pursuits group when we had surfed the waves on the wide beach and circumnavigated Ramsey Island in our fibreglass Perception kayaks, surrounded by seals. I was never much good at kayaking. I remember Mr Gilby saying to me after I'd capsized for the umpteenth time on a surf wave, 'Colin, you're not the best kayaker, but I take my hat off to your enthusiasm.' Those were formative, carefree and happy days.

~~~

Miles of fascinating rocky coastline ensued. Our speed gradually decreased as we reached Strumble Head. It was as though a switch had been flicked when the tide changed against us. In an instant, we had a battle on our hands and were forced to work like dogs. We had no wind to help us and were faced with a setting sun and no obvious sign of safe harbour. We had no choice but to make it to Fishguard.

It seemed that every day, like one of Nelson's ships of the line, we drew ourselves alongside the tide for a battle to the finish. Eddy hopping, ferry gliding and hard graft got us through, landing us on a tiny beach at Garn Wen, overlooking Fishguard harbour.

A flat piece of long grass, although heavily populated by midges, provided a good place for our tarp and a welcome place to rest. I received my first midge bite of 2017 – maybe they had been following us all the way from Scotland. Too tired to cook properly, we made a pan of porridge, our go-to food when all else failed. The following day, we planned to head to Cardigan Bay to see an old friend.

I made a phone call to Katrina, who had booked into a campsite at the top of the cliffs above Fishguard Bay. From where Davis and I were camped, I could see the lights of the campsite and, like children, we had fun signalling to each other with our headtorches across the mile-and-a-half expanse, chatting in the mild night air.

We made an early start the following day – a quick brew of salty coffee and we were off. Immediately, I was aware that before us lay a busy shipping area. The harbour entrance demanded caution as it was regularly used by ferries to Rosslare in southern Ireland. Davis spoke of these ships fondly. He knew them by name as he had been a frequent passenger on trips across the water.

Our destination that day was Llangrannog on Cardigan Bay, some 25 miles away. We were going well and knew we could cover this distance on one tide. Steady paddling, through deep coastal estuaries and a rugged coastline broken up by the odd golden beach, made for an enjoyable ride. The sandy beach at Llangrannog came into sight and we paddled in past protruding rocks. Waiting for us, smiling, were Katrina and Sue and Bill Taylor.

34 years had passed since Bill and I had last seen each other and I was surprised, given the number of people he has taught over the years, that he remembered me. He had hardly changed – his enthusiasm and charisma remained indomitable.

With forethought that only a practitioner could possess, Bill had brought a trailer to the beach for our canoe. He knew that we would want to keep it safe while we spent the rest of the day at his home.

Bill and Sue were the perfect hosts. They understood that we just needed a bit of looking after before we went back into the breach. Bill was genuinely excited about our trip and keen to hear all the details.

We spent a memorable evening with Bill, Sue and their son Jeff, reminiscing about our days at Thamesview school, the outdoor pursuits group and various teachers. Bill talked of his own UK and Ireland circumnavigation and his many subsequent expeditions across the world in canoes and kayaks and on horseback. This wonderfully relaxing day was rounded off with us all playing guitars and singing folk songs late into the evening.

Bill persuaded us to rest and spend the following day at his house. He believed that it would be good for us to re-charge our batteries, both electronic and physical, and carry out any necessary repairs. By this time, the hull of the canoe was showing some signs of wear, after being dragged up countless beaches of sand, pebbles and rocks over the previous 71 days, so I patched it up with lengths of KeelEazy tape. Everything else seemed to be holding up remarkably well, considering the strains to which they had been subjected.

Refreshed, we left the following morning in the rain. Bill, Sue and Katrina were on the beach to see us off. We said goodbye, took a final photo together and launched through a small surf. Our ambitious plan was to cross Cardigan Bay.

29

Island of the Currents

11ᵗʰ July 2017

Striking out boldly, we aimed for the tip of the Llyn Peninsula, 44 miles across Cardigan Bay. We were unclear as to where we would land but adopted an approach of 'get across the bay and then decide', although our favoured option was to land at Aberdaron.

The scene around us was dull and featureless, without horizon. We paddled through persistent heavy rain, which gradually filled the canoe. Our course was dictated by compass and GPS.

We chatted and felt at ease. The rest day had done us both the world of good. One thing, however, was playing on my mind. While we were at Bill's house, Davis and I had been offered a bottle of beer. Davis had readily accepted, but I had declined as I had been teetotal for ten years. I had seen a brief glimpse of disappointment in Bill's eyes as I turned down the offer. As we paddled away from the beach, I felt sad that I had not shared a drink with an old friend. In that moment, I vowed that the next time I saw Bill, or any old friend, I would never turn down a drink or two.

Tides came and went, leading to changes in our speed. Over the course of a crossing of this size, which would take over 12 hours, we knew that one tide would cancel the other out. So, when our speed dropped to 3 mph, we kept going in the knowledge that, in a few hours, the tide would turn again and help us home.

The wind gradually picked up during the day, but came from the north west, meaning that we made progress with close-hauled, tight sails. The force of the wind was creating leeway, and the canoe moved sideways as well as forwards. We managed to keep on a reasonable course, unaware of the pickle we were about to get ourselves into.

~~~

At sea, things can go wrong very quickly. We were approximately six miles from land, on a direct course for Aberdaron, when the wind suddenly changed to a brisk northeasterly and, despite us both paddling hard, the boat came to a standstill.

To our left was Bardsey Sound, a stretch of water between the tall cliffs of the Llyn Peninsula and the small island of Bardsey, the Island of the Currents. We were on a spring tide, and the water was flowing through this gap at a rate of eight knots. We knew that these strong currents could cause problems for any boat, but we thought this was to be an obstacle we would face the next day. We hadn't realised that, to land at Aberdaron, we would need to cross over the flow at the entrance to the Sound.

We tried to keep on course but were caught in the current, pulling us away from our destination. We changed direction using the wind, trying to gain headway, but even our best efforts failed to keep us from being dragged in. Davis and I shouted to one another to be heard above the noise of the wind and sea.

Aberdaron was disappearing out of sight and we were being sucked into the Sound as if into a black hole.

With one last effort, I angled the canoe into the current, caught as much wind as I could in the sails, and began to head off at an angle.

'NO! NO!' Davis shouted at the top of his voice. I couldn't understand why he didn't want to try this approach and continued with my plan.

Davis turned angrily to look at me, pointing ahead. 'LOOK!'

The sail had blocked my view. Looking underneath, I saw what Davis was concerned about. Ahead, a foaming tide race of huge spiralling, spinning waves had formed off the cliffs. We were heading into oblivion.

Between a rock and a hard place, we quickly turned about, heading away from the danger in front of us, towards Bardsey Island. Paddle-sailing as hard as we could, our progress was marginal. Left with no choice, we conceded to the current to run the gauntlet of Bardsey Sound.

Without sails or paddling, we were carried at a rate of 9 mph. The sea had become a river. Initially, this was a relief and a chance to re-gain our composure but, soon, a series of tide races developed within the Sound. Accepting our fate, we prepared for the imminent skirmishes and paddled.

After what seemed like an age of bouncing through the giant aquatic egg box, we seemed to have reached the westernmost corner of the Llyn Peninsula. We stopped, and, in the rocking canoe, checked our GPS, looking for a place to land. I noted that our speed was decreasing – 5 mph, 4 mph, 3 mph, 2 mph, 1 mph, 0 mph. We stopped. But then our speed picked back up again – 1 mph, 2 mph, 3 mph … we were being dragged backwards, back into the Sound. Things were becoming desperate.

We paddled with all our might. The sun was almost gone. More tide races threatened our safety until, eventually, we came in sight of a small beach. In the distance was the silhouette of a rock. I was sure it moved, but my eyesight isn't as good as it once was, so I asked Davis, 'Is that rock a boat?'

He replied, as surprised as me, 'Yeah, I think it's a canoe.'

In the dark, through the rough water, the canoeist paddled out to us, and a well-spoken voice called out, 'Hi, my name's Luke. We've been watching you from the clifftops going through the tide races. Absolutely fantastic. I so wanted to be out there with you!'

I thought, 'This guy is crazy!'

Luke pointed to a small white light coming from the shore. His Mum was shining a torch so that we would know where to land. As excited to see us as Luke had been, his Mum asked us if we'd like a cake. We didn't need asking twice. Within an hour, we were camped on the patio of a small beach café, eating cake and laughing about our 52-mile ordeal.

Katrina tells the observer's story of our Bardsey misadventure:

'After leaving Bill and Sue's house, I headed inland to visit Ray and Lina, who were excited to hear about the boys' adventure so far.

The evening was drawing on. Lina had gone to bed, and Ray was working in his office as I sat in the living room watching the orange dots of the Spot Messenger gradually work their way across the screen of my phone. It wouldn't be long before they landed at Aberdaron. The next dot surprised me – they were heading west. That hadn't been the plan.

It was like being in the NASA mission control room during a crisis as I stood in the doorway of Ray's office. He had been following the dots on his computer as he worked, and now we both tried to work out their plan as the next dot appeared, showing that they had travelled south west towards Bardsey Island.

Ten minutes passed. We waited for another dot to appear, but it didn't. 20 minutes, 30 minutes, 40 minutes … no dot. My stress was growing by the minute. I was worried. Suddenly, four new dots appeared on our screens. My knees nearly gave way with relief – they had made it through Bardsey Sound. Half an hour later, after the last dot appeared at Porth Oer, I received the "We're ok" message through the Spot Messenger. I could relax.'

30

Anglesey

12th – 15th July 2017

Once bitten, twice shy. I was nervous getting into the canoe the following morning. I didn't want another pounding – just an easy day to take us to the mouth of the Menai Strait.

Shortly after our departure, Luke paddled out to us in his red canoe. He was a fascinating person, as well as being one of the best paddlers I've ever come across. Luke can pole a canoe, gondolier fashion, up rapids that many people would struggle to descend. His other many talents include being a multi-instrument musician and an amazing woodcarver. He stayed with us for a few miles before presenting us with more cake and wishing us a safe onward journey.

A steady 25-mile paddle-sail took us to a long curving beach at Dinas Dinlle, near Caernarfon, where my sister, Kate was waiting for us. We spent a sunny afternoon planning for the next day and eating ice cream. After a fish and chip supper, we enjoyed a starry bivvy on the beach.

We started again at 7 am the following day. Navigating the canoe through sandbars proved a challenge as we entered the mouth of the Menai Strait. Our aim for the day was to reach the north coast of Anglesey over two tides. I had considered going around the south of the island but decided against it. We were near spring tides and, having previously experienced the tide races off Penrhyn Mawr and South Stack, neither Davis nor I was in the mood for this trial. Our other option, journeying in the sheltered waters of the Menai Strait, was much more inviting. The strait is a narrow stretch of water separating the island of Anglesey from mainland Wales. Its strong tidal waters are complex but can provide a welcome push if a journey through them is timed well. Time them badly on a route, and you're stuck.

~~~

The last time I had been through the fast-flowing waters of the Menai Strait was two years previous to this. In early June 2015, aided by good weather, Katrina and I found ourselves heading to Cemlyn Bay on the north coast of Anglesey, where we would start our circumnavigation of the island.

Our canoe for this bold expedition was our Penobscot, fitted with a small expedition sail and a partial homemade canvas spray deck.

At 7 am, we paddled out of the calm waters of Cemlyn Bay.

We had spent hours studying the tidal flow charts and knew that we had three hours to get past Penrhyn Mawr before the tide turned against us. I kept telling myself, 'Keep to the plan, we'll be alright.'

As we left the bay, helpful tidal waters ferried us along. There was no wind, the sky was clear, and it promised to be a hot day. Almost immediately, in the distance, I saw white caps stretching out to sea from the shore. With no wind, this could only mean one thing – a tide race. This didn't bode well as, by my calculations, the waters would be calm at this point.

We had never encountered a tide race before, and we were now committed as the swell rose into smooth steep waves – just enough for us to handle. Nervously, we laughed as the canoe slapped and plunged bow first into the troughs. Occasionally, the crest of a wave collapsed around us.

Time was running out. We needed to maintain a speed of 5 mph, and, without wind, this meant hard graft with the paddles. We passed The Skerries to our right as we cut the corner towards North Stack on Holy Island. We were becoming more relaxed, and the subsequent tide races were fun – we paddled hard along wave trains, enjoying the exciting ride. To our left were the white cliffs of Gogarth, where I had previously spent days climbing and scaring myself silly on the sea-washed rock.

Our three hours were nearly up when we arrived at Penrhyn Mawr, the last tide race of this section. Here, we made a mistake. Thinking we had the passage in the bag, we were complacent. From nowhere came a rude awakening. In an instant, the tide turned, and we realised that the flow was against us. 20 metres in front of us, a breaking standing wave formed. We were so close to sanctuary but were stuck. I couldn't bear the thought of retreating at this point, and we paddled frantically, without moving, trying to find a way through. Moving to our right seemed to be our best bet, but all the time the waves were increasing. With a supreme effort of frantic paddling, we just managed to get past the standing waves but promptly became stuck on a river of water.

Our efforts were futile. We had no option but to turn around. Suddenly, I felt a cool breeze on the back of my neck and shouted:

'Kat, get the sail up!'

'I can't hear you!'

'SAIL ... UP!'

Trembling through a surge of adrenaline and fumbling to find the ropes, Katrina pulled up the lugsail, and the boat started moving forwards. It was as though we had a fresh pair of paddles, and, gradually, we escaped the clutches of the tide. A short time later, we stopped at the welcoming beach of Trearddur Bay.

After waiting for the tide to turn, we continued our journey. We paddled through the Menai Strait in the dark and set up camp next to the road at Gallows Point at 2.30 am.

By 8 am, we were back in the canoe. Paddle-sailing easily with the tide, we encountered more tide races – the biggest we had ever seen. Relaxed, we laughed and shouted 'Yee-haa!' as we stormed through vertical corniced waves. Eventually, the wind died down, and we paddled gently through the sunset to Cemlyn Bay.

This journey confirmed to me that the circumnavigation of the UK was possible.

~~~

With Davis, paddling in the sunshine along the enclosed Menai Strait felt like a stress-free holiday. Caernarfon Castle dominated the scene at the western end. Further along, the remarkable statue of Nelson and the Britannia Bridge, as well as the Menai Suspension Bridge, provided interesting views. The paddling was made easier by the strong currents, which showed their hand in the tidal rapids of the Swellies. These were flowing nicely, and we both enjoyed bouncing through their white waves. It was fun and I felt at home and comfortable.

We landed on the rocky beach of Lleiniog, near Penmon on the southeastern tip of Anglesey, excited to have seen bottlenose dolphins. We were met by Paul Airy, a fellow canoeist and friend of Bill Taylor. Bill had asked Paul to look out for us. Paul and his wife were very welcoming, and together we enjoyed lunch overlooking the strait before setting off on the afternoon tide.

Paddling toward Puffin Island was easy, but, after turning to follow the eastern coast of Anglesey, the headwind gained strength. Our sails became useless, and only with Davis and I working hard and digging in with our paddles did we move. The wind against the tide made for steep waves, and we shipped water. I couldn't help but think, 'here we go again'.

At this point, my navigation went astray and, prompted by Davis, I realised that I couldn't make out fine features on the map or land. I don't think Davis was reassured when I told him I needed to get some glasses.

To Davis's exasperation and my embarrassment, my navigational blunder had left us over a mile from our planned destination of Porth Eilian. Back on course, slogging through waves and wind as we headed to the point, a yacht bounced over to us and drew alongside.

The skipper looked as though he had seen a pair of aliens. With the puzzled expression of someone who couldn't make sense of what he was looking at, he asked, 'You guys ok?'

'We're fine thanks, just going around the UK.'

~~~

The final plan of our UK circumnavigation was a bold one. We intended to strike a course almost directly home through the Irish Sea. On leaving Anglesey, we would paddle-sail to the Isle of Man. From there, we would cross to Northern Ireland before heading back to Scotland and home.

I have often been asked why we chose this route, instead of sticking to the west coast of England. The reason was a combination of fear, common sense and adventure.

The waters around the coastline from Liverpool to the south Lake District are shallow, and navigation would be difficult, as would camping. On our planned route, we would give the notorious tide races off the Mull of Galloway and the Mull of Kintyre a wide berth. Crossing the Irish Sea had an adventurous feel about it. We enjoyed big crossings, and I had always fancied going to the Isle of Man. In addition, the trip would allow us to catch up with a few people along the way – Jude and Bill Todd, the owners of Downcreek (now Freebird) Paddles, live in Belfast and we wanted to see them and show them how their paddles had held up. It was also an opportunity for Davis to see his Dad en route.

Taking our planned route would, however, mean saying goodbye to Katrina. For the remaining 300 or so miles, we would be fending for ourselves.

Leaving Katrina was a necessary but difficult psychological hurdle. Katrina had supported the idea of the trip from its origins years before and spent a massive amount of time researching and sourcing the right canoe and equipment for the trip. She had worked out how much food, how many batteries and what spare clothing we needed to take with us on each leg. We planned the route together and spent hours discussing contingencies. She worked out the logistics of how she would support Davis and me while also looking after herself and our two dogs.

For the previous 75 days, Katrina had been on hand if we needed her. If we had nowhere to camp, we slept in the van, often waking her in the early hours as we rose and prepared for another day at sea. She had run about buying food, replacing broken equipment, charging batteries and washing our smelly clothes. She kept people updated by phone and internet, often making contact with the coastguard on our behalf when we had no phone or VHF signal. Before each leg, she would ring ahead, trying to find a secure place for us to keep our canoe and somewhere for us to stay or camp. Katrina was the unsung hero of the whole expedition – the ground control who put the astronauts on the moon.

For two days, strong northerly winds kept us in Porth Eilian. We used this time to prepare the canoe, replenish our food and water supplies, and relax. We knew we were nearly home, but, with some vast crossings and dangerous waters still to navigate, we were acutely aware that completion wasn't a formality.

31

The Isle of Man

16th – 17th July 2017

On Sunday 16th July, the winds eased and blew from the east. Conditions were good for us to go. At 8 am, we said goodbye to Katrina and paddled out from the shelter of Porth Eilian into the Irish Sea. The Isle of Man, our destination, was out of sight. The day was a complete contrast to our struggle of three days beforehand – the wind was helpful and the canoe rode the sea without losing speed. The day blossomed into one of beautiful sunshine as, gradually, the long, faint silhouette of the Isle of Man came into view – although it didn't appear to get any closer.

Despite excellent paddling conditions and stunning weather, sitting in the canoe hour after hour was uncomfortable, and the paddling was continuous and monotonous. For most of the trip, we were lucky to have the mostly beautiful UK coastline and its constantly changing panoramas to divert our minds from the task at hand. To break the toil, we had a routine which had developed naturally. In good conditions, we usually paddle-sailed for an hour and then drifted for five minutes having a drink and a bite to eat.

Early starts dulled our appetites, making breakfast unpalatable, so we generally postponed the first meal of the day until we were well underway, eating and drinking in the canoe. Before any leg of the journey, I made a small flask of coffee for each of us. This came to be known as our salty coffee, as the flask inevitably gained a few splashes of added seawater. This flask was easily accessible and we held it in a bike drinks holder. To supplement this on longer crossings, I made up two larger flasks of black tea. Water was always to hand.

I became excited by small things – anything to break up the monotony. A simple jellyfish was a source of wonder – a fragile, otherworldly creature pulsing effortlessly through the water. Occasionally, we would see huge, colourful barrel jellyfish – the perfect name for these monsters of the jelly world, with diameters of up to two feet. When a porpoise or dolphin surfaced, our excitement often caused us to stop and search the sea for more.

For entertainment, seabirds were excellent value. I was in awe of the shearwater's ability to fly just inches above the waves. Gannets are my favourite bird – beautiful and graceful, often operating in squadrons, heads tilting as if looking for their targets. I imagine them talking to one another in 1940s upper-class voices, like Second World War RAF pilots:

'Gannet One, this is Gannet Leader. Over.'

'Go ahead, Gannet Leader.'

'Mackerel shoal at 12 o'clock. Over.'

'Roger that, Gannet Leader, I'm going in.'

Puffins were very common in places. More than any other type of bird, they evoke feelings of sympathy. Their colourful yet sorrowful faces, round bodies, ungainly flight and crash landings made them endearing to the spectator. If we disturbed a floating puffin as we paddled past, it usually either dived or tried to take off. We found ourselves egging them on, encouraging them in their desperate attempts at flight as they flapped and bounced along the waves, in a desperate attempt to become airborne.

One bird I found fascinatingly sinister was the great skua, or bonksie, as they are otherwise known. We had only come across these in the northern parts of Scotland. They are large, thick-set seagull-type birds with a mottled brown but attractive plumage. They would follow our canoe for miles, and I felt like a weak wildebeest being stalked by a vulture. Like avian thugs, muggers of the sky, they attack other birds such as gannets. In flight, they would grab the wing of their prey and cause it to crash land into the sea, where they would force it to regurgitate its recently caught fish or drown it.

The coastline of the UK is a good place to daydream, influenced as it is by history from so many time periods. Scattered artefacts, ancient harbours, forts and castles offer glimpses of times long past. In the canoe, I could, for brief spells, drift back in time and imagine that I was looking at the land as my ancestors did. Gazing at the Isle of Man, lying low and hazy on the horizon, no towns visible and too far away to discern any human interference with the land, I thought of this as a view shared by countless mariners through the ages.

Our canoe continued to move purposefully through the sea, and we were soon able to make out the towns along the coast. Our destination was Douglas, the seaside capital of the island.

We gave the harbour at Douglas a wide berth and landed on the beach in front of the hotel-lined town. As we landed, a couple who had been following our progress greeted us with a smile. They offered to help, and I gave them some money to buy us fish and chips while we carried our equipment up the long, flat, sandy beach.

It was then that I received a panicked call from Katrina, telling me to ring the harbour master. It transpired that someone had been following our progress on the live Spot Messenger link and wrongly assumed that we had landed in the harbour. A phone call had been made to the harbour master, who could not find us and was at the point of raising the alarm. Our friend Greg had picked up on the problem via a message on Facebook. I made a quick call to the harbour master to let him know that all was well.

This was a danger associated with making our Spot Messenger tracking public on social media. This example was a case of genuine concern, but miscommunication had potential to set the hares running unnecessarily. For this reason, in subsequent adventures, I only gave a select few people access to my tracking, and now do not make it public until after the event.

~~~

A lazy midday start the next day saw us paddling along a rocky coast, broken intermittently by sandy beaches and towns made up of white houses.

Our transit was eased by light winds, which died as we crossed Ramsey Bay, leaving us with a hot slog. Unconcerned, we paddled to the north tip of the island, which was marked by a red and white lighthouse. A pebbly beach stretched for miles and provided us with a good landing spot. We camped in a green meadow protected by a shingle dune. It had been an easy day, with just one 24-mile stretch on clear blue water, leaving us in an ideal position to cross to Northern Ireland.

Davis and I chatted with the outlines of Northern Ireland and Scotland faintly visible in the distance as the sun descended into the sea below a bright orange sky. Tensions between Davis and I had steadily been evaporating since we had left the south coast of England. As we lay in this meadow, we were relaxed in each other's company.

32

Northern Ireland

18th – 21st July 2017

Dawn was breaking. Nearly 50 miles away, out of sight, lay our destination – the small seaside town of Donaghadee in County Down. A southeasterly wind was blowing perfectly, and the one-and-a-half metre swell was manageable.

Paddling away from the shore, we saw the two distinct fins of a basking shark above the surface of the water, silhouetted in the sunrise. The Isle of Man is famous for these massive, gentle, plankton-eating sharks. This time, though, we had no time to stop and the early morning light made observation difficult, so we continued on our way.

As we neared the North Channel, where the Irish Sea separates Northern Ireland from Scotland, the seas began to rise. Strong tidal currents combined with the wind to make the surface of the sea difficult for a canoe to handle. White horses were evident in all directions as both the wind speed and swell size increased. Out came the bailing bucket, which, for all its simplicity, was one of the most essential pieces of our equipment.

At this stage in our journey, Davis and I were not easily intimidated, but, with the breaking swell running behind us, our nerve was tested. It was essential to keep our speed down so that waves would flow under the canoe. Going too fast would run the risk of us being picked up by a wave and surfing out of control. I laughed to myself as, often, I would try to slow the boat down by reducing the sail area, but Davis would continue to paddle fast and hard.

As we approached Donaghadee, my phone buzzed in my pocket – such is life on a 21st-century adventure. It was Jude, telling me that Bangor would be a good place to land – only another two miles along the coast. By this time, though, the tide had turned against us and it was difficult to make any headway. Two more miles at this speed would take over two hours, and we'd already been on the go for over eight hours. I politely declined Jude's request – we would stick to plan A.

The first bay we reached at Donaghadee had very little beach and nowhere to camp. Reluctantly, we climbed back into the canoe and paddled to a slipway a short distance away, near a sailing club. Jude and Bill were there to meet us, along with Davis's Dad, Sean, and his step-brother, little Sean. It was great to see friends and family, and we set about emptying our canoe of equipment.

We learned that a crew from Ulster TV wanted to interview us. The presenter was a young woman wearing smart clothing and with an overpowering aroma of perfume. She seemed to exist in stark contrast to Davis and me, who had been wearing the same clothes for three long hot days on the water, and hadn't shaved for weeks. Although we were exhausted, we were happy to take part in the interview – until she asked us to get back into the canoe and paddle out to sea so that her cameraman could get some action footage. After our 48-mile paddle across the Irish Sea, we didn't react well to her request! Sulking, with our heads down and slumped shoulders, we stomped away, dragged the boat back down the slip and did as requested. The footage was priceless – two more grim-faced, angry-looking paddlers you could not imagine.

The local sailing club was fantastic. They allowed us to camp, use their facilities and leave our canoe in their boatyard. Friendly Irish canoe activist Big Al took us to one of the oldest pubs in Belfast before we retired to our tarp, pitched neatly between two dinghies.

We planned to head north the following day and get into a good position to cross the North Channel back to Scotland. This would keep us clear of the tide races which run off the tip of the Mull of Kintyre.

Following a sleepless, windy night listening to the rattle and hum of sailboat rigging, we paddled along towards the entrance of Belfast harbour. Like Pavlov's dog, crossing any big harbour set my adrenal glands working overtime. This was no exception, as it was the unwelcome territory of big ships.

Cautiously, we made our way across the seven-mile-wide harbour entrance, stopping on several occasions to let gigantic vessels pass. Across the harbour, we paddle-sailed past the remarkable Gobbins Cliff Path, a high-rise walkway hanging off the side of the cliff. The sea was not without interest, and, for stability and my nerves, we only used one small sail. Despite the good wind, though, we continued to paddle – almost a reflex for us.

Glenarm, a beautiful quiet seaside town in a small bay surrounded by colourful, neatly painted houses was our next destination. The unbelievably helpful harbour master rallied round people in the village, and we soon found ourselves billeted in the Glenarm Rowing Club clubhouse. A short time later, we were sitting in a quiet café with wooden tables, enjoying coffee and a bun with Jude. Returning to the clubhouse, we found a local member of the rowing club, Roy, who offered to cook us tea and put us up for the night, which we readily accepted.

With the Mull of Kintyre in our sights, we set off at 9 am the following day. In the flattish, sheltered waters of Glenarm, paddling and assisted by a good southwesterly wind, we reached incredible speeds of up to 9 mph, sending our leeboard into a hum. Gradually, our speed decreased to a steady 5 mph. As if we were crossing a huge road, our time was spent calculating whether or not we were on a collision course with the big ships that patrolled this waterway like giant blind dinosaurs.

As we neared the bulk of the Mull of Kintyre peninsula, our speed slowed and the wind died. We had crossed the North Channel, but here the waters boiled, lifting our canoe, and the swell began to grow. Sensing a massive amount of latent energy in the sea, Davis and I paddled hard to escape. We were soon struggling to keep the canoe moving at 2 mph, and we realised that the tide was against us. Our best option was to head to the east Mull of Kintyre coast to escape the current. Keeping tight to the shore, we spent the last couple of miles eddy hopping, being careful not to be dumped onto the rocks by the clear blue breaking swell.

We located a safe place to land through a reef at the edge of Machrihanish, a small town with a beach famed for its surfing. We contemplated the fact that, in May, a surfer had been swept out to sea here by the strong tides. He was rescued 13 miles off the coast of Northern Ireland, after spending 32 hours adrift.

The following day, strong winds accompanied by torrential rain dictated a day of rest in our damp tent. We relaxed, happy enough, as the forecast was improving.

Next to the quiet road, we attracted some attention, resulting in an interview with the local newspaper and a visit from the nearby canoe club, who came to see us off the following morning.

33

Gulfs, Firths and Sounds

22nd – 23rd July 2017

Davis and I wanted to get home. We were both tired and knew that, barring a catastrophe, the circumnavigation was in the bag. We still had well over 100 miles left, and we reckoned that we could cover this in just three days.

Our departure from Machrihanish went smoothly, the strong pulling tide as impressive as the surf on the beach. Crossing the entrance to Loch Caolisport, though, our hopes of an easy day were shattered. A gusty and unhelpful wind, coupled with a long fetch from the loch, drove oncoming waves, almost as big as any we had encountered. In the ensuing maelstrom, we dropped our noisily flapping sails and paddled with a determination usually reserved for situations of near disaster.

Thankfully, shelter from the wind at the Point of Knap was not far away, and, gradually, we left the big waves behind us, but then the tide turned. We were in for another hard day. Eddy hopping close to the shore, we set ourselves small objectives of islands and headlands until, eventually, relieved, we called it a day and stopped on the small island of Danna.

I was smitten with the Sound of Jura – an enchanting place. Mysterious islands and dark mountains line this beautiful waterway flowing between mainland Scotland and the islands of Islay, Jura and Scarba. It is home to strong spring tides, which form mini-rapids and over-falls.

Our campsite was ideal – flat and almost midge-free. A major crisis, though, had happened ... we were out of coffee. To make matters worse, I was rationing tea bags – four cups out of one bag. Despite this monumental logistical problem, Davis and I relaxed into our well-established camp routine of putting up the tent and cooking.

Content with our day's effort, I was dropping off to sleep when my mind drifted to a quote I had once heard. A mountaineer had been sitting in base camp at the foot of a mountain in perfect conditions, and, when asked why he wasn't climbing, said, 'I know I can do it so why bother?'

Struck by this thought, I asked, 'Davis, what do you think people would say if we just stopped now and said "we knew we could do it, so we didn't bother?"' We laughed and went to sleep.

The next day, we knew that the tide would be against us for at least six hours, but we kept going. We had contemplated not stopping until we reached home, but decided against this as the risks of paddling exhausted at night were too high. Our route would take us through some sections of water with powerful currents, especially in a spring tide.

Looking at the maps, we both agreed that reaching Oban would mean covering a good distance that day, but we wanted to go further. We decided to aim for Lochaline, some 40 miles away for us, but only a short drive from Strontian. Although, on leaving Anglesey, we had not expected to see Katrina again until we arrived home, I called and asked her to meet us there with clean clothes and coffee.

At 7 am, we cruised through a sheltered calm bay into the narrowing Sound of Jura. Ahead and to our left, about four miles away, lay the long island of Jura with the island of Scarba visible to the north. The gap between the two islands is the Gulf of Corryvreckan, home to the famous Corryvreckan Whirlpool, caused by the fast-flowing tide through the narrow gap. A dangerous vortex and five-metre standing waves are created, the subject of legend and folklore for centuries. Our route would take us close to this hazard as we left the Sound of Jura and entered the narrow, fast-flowing, Sound of Luing.

Initially, the tide was against us, so we tucked in close to the shore, but soon it turned in our favour. Riffles, boils and tiny over-falls indicated where the current was at its strongest, so we aimed for these. The paddling was fun, like going down an easy river. With very little wind, it was nice to have some assistance from the sea.

To our right lay Loch Craignish. Water flowing out of here into the Sound of Jura added to the complications of the tides in this area. Looming to our left like a black hole was the Gulf of Corryvreckan. The canoeing was as good as canoeing gets and, with interesting currents, we made good speed past beautiful small skerries in the clear dark-blue sea, beneath a pale blue sky with the odd solitary cotton wool cloud. We were alone – hardly a sign of another human on land or sea for miles.

With the memory of being swept through Bardsey Sound fresh in my mind, we reached the mouth of the Gulf of Corryvreckan. Adrenaline pumped through my body and our cadence picked up because I could feel the tidal flow of the Corryvreckan sucking us towards what we were convinced would be oblivion.

Two miles later, we were clear, looking forward to a free ride and being swept through the Sound of Luing, but it didn't happen. We managed a speed of 4 mph, paddling with a light wind in our sails, but we should have been much faster.

Gradually, though, our speed picked up as the sea around us showed signs of tidal movement in our favour. Midway down the sound, we began to see the tell-tale white edges of small over-falls and riffles and our speed increased to a satisfying 10 mph.

Before us, a yacht of around 30 feet in length was trying to travel against the strong current. With water flowing into its bows, it was struggling, stationary, swinging from left to right as the engine tried its best to move the boat forward. Nearing the yacht, Davis and I watched with that annoying 'this could be interesting' expressions of people waiting for something to go wrong. We did, though, have the decency not to film the incident on our mobile phones. The skipper's persistence was gradually rewarded as the yacht made headway. We continued on our way, wondering why a skipper would want to take his boat against such a current, and followed a small tide race and whirlpools into the Firth of Lorn.

The tide was due to turn against us. We planned to cross the firth and gain shelter from the tide by hugging the south coast of Mull. The wind coming from the north east enabled us to paddle-sail across to the island. As good as this was, we knew that, when we arrived at the coast, we would be heading into the wind and tide. Over the next few hours, I knew we were going to suffer.

The canoe moved slowly along the rocky shoreline against a strong wind. On occasion, the boat ground to a halt, requiring a mighty effort to re-gain forward momentum. Hugging the shore helped to keep us out of the tide and gave us more shelter from the oncoming waves and swell, but also increased the risk of us being picked up and shipwrecked on the rocks.

Davis and I had several disagreements about the best way to go. Davis wanted to get close in to the shore, but I preferred to keep out a little and accept stronger currents and bigger waves.

We were too close to finishing to risk the boat and completion of the circumnavigation.

The ten miles we travelled along this coast was one of the hardest pieces of paddling I have ever done. My whole body ached. My shoulder muscles felt like over-tightened knots, my legs were on the verge of cramp, and my back was a source of constant dull pain. We couldn't stop as this would mean going backwards. Already very tired after 30 miles of canoeing, we were on a hill of Alpine proportions. Our only salvation was the knowledge that, when we turned into the Sound of Mull, the wind would be in our favour.

There was a temptation to stop in the shelter of Lochs Spelve and Don, but that would be admitting defeat, so we carried on into the darkness. Eventually, after the grimmest of paddling struggles, we turned into the Sound of Mull, but our day still wasn't over.

At last, the wind came to our assistance, but a formidable tide was still against us. As often happens, the wind cancelled out the tide, and we made a steady 3 mph, paddle-sailing on a bearing into Lochaline.

From a distance I saw a flashing torch. Katrina was waiting for us on the beach. It had been an utterly exhausting day – 45 miles, 16 hours, no stops and nature's elements often against us. Davis and I stumbled out of the canoe like a pair of Saturday night drunks. We climbed into the van, exhausted.

34

The Home Straight

24th July 2017

Monday 24th July 2017 – we were on the home straight. 15 miles of paddling would see us close the circle at the point on Loch Sunart we had left 86 days earlier.

We wanted to catch a tide that would carry us down Loch Sunart, and achieving this in one day meant starting against the flow on the Sound of Mull. It was a gloriously sunny and breezy day. As well as having the tide against us, a headwind also hindered our progress. We weren't bothered – it would only be for 12 miles and then we would turn the corner into Loch Sunart, where we would have both wind and tide pushing us home.

Michael, who we had met in Aberdeen, had travelled to Strontian the night before and driven to Lochaline that morning to see us off. We waved goodbye to him and Katrina as, for the last time, Davis and I climbed into the canoe and paddled out into the familiar dark-blue water. She gave this account of our departure:

'I watched as the boys paddled away from Lochaline then took a deep breath as I enjoyed the last brief moments of peace and tranquillity before returning home to Strontian, where Colin and Davis's family had gathered. I was finding it difficult to deal with. I'd spent the majority of the last three months alone, just my dogs and me, no one fussing and no expectations. Suddenly, I found myself feeling like a guest in my own home. Colin would be home that evening, and yet we would sleep in the van on the road outside our house as all the rooms were taken.'

Davis and I paddled close to the shore. We knew that the day would be a slog to start with, but we were distracted from our efforts by the undeniable beauty of the scene around us. The majestic Ardnamurchan peninsula was in full view. Kilchoan, where we had stopped on our first night, was just discernible in the distance. Several yachts heeled over amongst white horses as they sailed to Tobermory. The Morvern shore to our right offered continual interest, and a close-up display from a white-tailed eagle enhanced our already good mood.

At Auliston Point, the junction of Loch Sunart with the Sound of Mull, we gradually turned the canoe to face east and raised the sails. The tide and wind combined their natural forces to drive us home. 20 minutes later, I checked the GPS. We had closed the circle, and our journey around the UK was complete. All that remained was a swift paddle-sail home to Strontian.

I wanted to mark the moment, and so I leaned forward to shake Davis's hand, saying, 'We did it, mate!'

Davis was smiling. 'Cheers, Colin.'

It all felt a bit anti-climactic.

We continued past Glenborrodale, where we were joined by a friend from Yorkshire, Onno, who had paddled out to meet us in a borrowed sea kayak. He surfed the waves beside us as we sailed towards Strontian. We didn't have far to go when Michael joined us, paddling a canoe.

We had seen Ellen MacArthur signalling her record-breaking round the world trip with the use of marine safety flares and had thought that this would be a good way to mark our arrival in Strontian. However, as our final landing spot came into view, we decided against this, thinking that it would be too pretentious. This was fortunate, as we were to discover later that Katrina had informed the coastguard of our plans to be told in no uncertain terms that flares must not be set off in these circumstances.

We pulled into the edge of the loch, next to the show field, the same spot we had launched from 86 days previously, to be met by a small group of friends, family, well-wishers from the village and, of course, Tyke and Gonzo. It was perfect, with hugs and handshakes all around. All that was left to do now was to put the canoe on the trolley and wheel her home.

Later that evening, Davis and I toasted our success with a wee dram of malt whisky – my first alcoholic drink in ten years.

Epilogue

Ray had warned me of post-expedition depression. I had listened to him but dismissed the thought. I recalled the many difficult situations I had been through as a police officer. I had never suffered depression through these times, so a canoe trip surely wouldn't cause me any problems. It turned out, however, that I was very wrong.

Immediately after our return, Davis spent a few days in Scotland before returning to Ireland to get his life back on track. With our friends and family departed, Katrina and I were left in a quiet void.

With the successful completion of the journey, the stress of the whole venture came to an abrupt end. I felt a weight of responsibility lifted from my shoulders. I had experienced an intense 86 days of life and death decision making. Davis and I had pushed boundaries and been in the spotlight on a journey that could have ended in disaster.

Almost immediately, I began to feel very flat about the whole experience. I was critical of both myself and Davis over very small incidents on the trip. I thought we had relied on

Katrina too much and should have been supported less. I felt disappointed that we hadn't raised more money for charity, but our focus had been on the journey and not on fundraising. Amongst all this, the reality of my retirement and loss of identity was kicking in. I hadn't had time to dwell on this before as planning the trip had been all-consuming. Now, I needed time to adjust to normality.

Before the trip, I had agreed to write an article for The Paddler magazine about our adventures. My heart wasn't in it, but I had made a commitment which I would keep. It wasn't easy as I didn't feel inspired. After it had been published, I cringed at my sloppy writing and found that I was losing self-confidence.

My change in mood was very subtle and unnoticeable to most.

Searching for meaning, I was keen that this trip didn't become something vaguely talked about but gradually forgotten. I volunteered to give talks about our adventure, knowing that public speaking would be good for me, a chance to re-gain lost confidence.

Tom Sibbald, a highly regarded canoeist, was keen for me to give the main presentation at the English Canoe Symposium in November 2017. He was working near our home and came over to chat about the possibility. I was happy to do a presentation but explained that neither Davis nor I were expert canoeists and had minimal qualifications.

He laughed and said, 'All you need to canoe around Britain is a good forward stroke. Anything more than that and you're over-qualified!'

Soon after this, Paul Kirtley, the owner of Frontier Bushcraft and an expert in his field, got in touch with me. We arranged to record an interview via Skype for Paul's highly acclaimed podcast series. Paul was fantastic, but I wasn't comfortable with the interview and found that I was self-critical of my answers for weeks afterwards.

Over the next year, I went on to give many presentations to different audiences, from canoeists to schoolchildren – an audience of 20 at Katrina's Mum's church to a standing-room only talk at the English Canoe Symposium. Some of these went better than others, but I felt that doing the talks gave meaning to our expedition.

Davis and I received the John MacGregor Outstanding Challenge Award, presented to us at the British Canoeing Awards evening along with two custom-made buoyancy aids from Peak UK. This wasn't the only recognition that Davis and I were granted. We were presented with a beautiful silver plate by the organisers of the West Ardnamurchan Regatta, and a lovely wooden trophy by the Open Canoe Sailing Group. I was also given a fantastic banner made by my ex-colleagues at West Yorkshire Police and Calderdale Council, who had followed our journey.

In 2018 I was awarded an MBE for 'services to policing and the community in Halifax.' After the investiture, Katrina and I were hosted in Westminster by the young and talented Holly Lynch, MP for Halifax. She had been a keen supporter of both our journey and the work of the emergency services.

Over time, life has returned to normal, and my view of the trip has evolved. Now, I can look back at photos, videos and my diary entries and be quietly pleased with our endeavour. I look at maps of the UK, and I realise the enormity of what Davis and I achieved. I feel very fortunate to have seen our stunning coastline and wildlife at close quarters. Yes, there were things that we could have done differently and perhaps better, but this no longer detracts from my satisfaction in completing such a journey.

My appreciation of Davis is immeasurable. Without him, the circumnavigation of the UK would not have happened. I could not have asked for a fitter, tougher or more resilient partner. He was outstanding in so many ways, and together we made an exceptional team. Yes, we disagreed over some decisions, and, on occasion, we sulked and just about tolerated each other, but we always shared a grim determination to finish. We have both been asked if there was ever a moment when we wanted to quit, and the answer has always been a definite 'No'. For two people to be in such close proximity to one another, under extreme stress, for three months, it is remarkable how well we got on together. Davis is more than family to me – he is a great friend.

My desire to push myself and see what's around the next corner is ever-present. In 2018, Katrina and I paddled to the remote Scottish islands of St Kilda. Lying 42 miles off the Western Isles of Scotland in the Atlantic Ocean, this remote archipelago had previously been reached by sea kayak but never an open canoe. In 2019, Katrina and I attempted the first crossing of the North Sea from Humberston, near Cleethorpes, to Den Helder in the Netherlands. We failed, but, after 100 miles and 29 hours at sea, I'm positive about the experience, which was a real adventure and leaves me with another story to tell.

Plenty of great canoe journeys and adventures, then, are still out there for anyone who wants one – it just takes a map and a little imagination.

Acknowledgments

I would not have been able to write this book if I had not had the adventure. I give thanks to my parents, Alan and Brenda, from the bottom of my heart, for giving me such an amazing childhood where I was encouraged to pursue my dreams, and for supporting me throughout my life no matter how crazy my ideas were. And to all the teachers involved in the outdoor pursuits group at Thamesview High School; two of these have been named within the book, but there were others who have not been mentioned, all of whom I also owe a debt of gratitude, in particular Bev Taylor and Len Thompson.

I would like to thank friends and family who have helped in the production of this book. Ted and Barbara Rotchell for bringing their red pens out of retirement and 'marking' the 'first final draft'. Simon and Liz Willis for their much appreciated help and advice, and for giving me hope that I was capable of writing something worth reading, and also for helping to choose the photographs. Sylvia Hehir for her encouragement and guidance through the post-writing stage in order that my words could become a tangible product.

My Editor, Alison Chand was superb, bringing much needed clarity to the book. And again, thank you Bill Taylor for allowing me to use the glossary of terms from *Commitment and Open Crossings.*

Finally, but most importantly, I could not have done any of this without my wonderful wife, my soulmate Katrina. Not only was she there every step along the journey, but she has put so much of her time into supporting me afterwards, listening to countless presentations and reading through seemingly endless drafts and helping to bring my story to life.

Appendix I
Map of Route

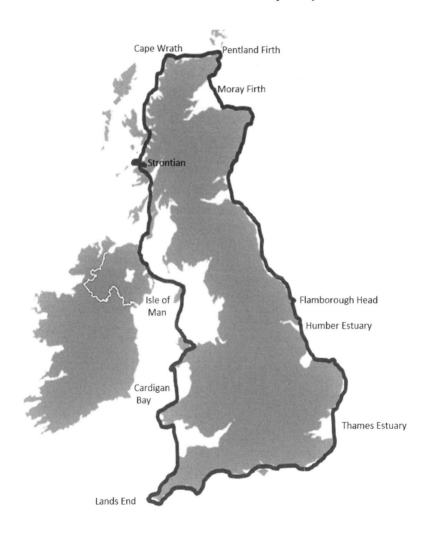

Cape Wrath

Pentland Firth

Moray Firth

Strontian

Isle of Man

Flamborough Head

Humber Estuary

Cardigan Bay

Thames Estuary

Lands End

Appendix II
Mileage Chart

Day	Date	Start	End	Miles	Total Miles
1	30 April	Strontian	Kilchoan	22.7	22.7
2	1 May	Kilchoan	Armadale (Skye)	34.1	56.8
3	2 May	Armadale (Skye)	Skye Bridge	21.9	78.7
4	3 May	Skye Bridge	Port Henderson	32.2	110.9
5	4 May	Port Henderson	Rubha Ruidh	15.3	126.2
6	5 May	Rubha Ruidh	Old Dornie	21	147.2
7	6 May	Old Dornie	Scourie	27.3	174.5
8	7 May	REST DAY	REST DAY	0	174.5
9	8 May	Scourie	Cnoc Garbh	11.7	186.2
10	9 May	Cnoc Garbh	Durness	24.7	210.9
11	10 May	Durness	Scrabster	48.8	259.7
12	11 May	REST DAY	REST DAY	0	259.7
13	12 May	REST DAY	REST DAY	0	259.7
14	13 May	REST DAY	REST DAY	0	259.7
15	14 May	Scrabster	Wick	38.1	297.8
16	15 May	REST DAY	REST DAY	0	297.8
17	16 May	REST DAY	REST DAY	0	297.8
18	17 May	Wick	Berriedale	25.4	323.2
19	18 May	Berriedale	Findochty	40.9	364.1
20	19 May	Findochty	Rattray Head	44.9	409
21	20 May	Rattray Head	Port Errol	15.7	424.7
22	21 May	Port Errol	Aberdeen	24.4	449.1

Day	Date	Start	End	Miles	Total Miles
23	22 May	Aberdeen	Gourdon	26.5	475.6
24	23 May	Gourdon	Arbroath	26.7	502.3
25	24 May	Arbroath	Skateraw	41.2	543.5
26	25 May	Skateraw	Berwick-upon-Tweed	30.1	573.6
27	26 May	REST DAY	REST DAY	0	573.6
28	27 May	REST DAY	REST DAY	0	573.6
29	28 May	Berwick-upon-Tweed	Boulmer	31.8	605.4
30	29 May	Boulmer	Roker	37.5	642.9
31	30 May	Roker	Whitby	45.9	688.8
32	31 May	Whitby	Bridlington Harbour	45.2	734
33	1 June	Bridlington Harbour	Bridlington Sailing Club	1.7	735.7
34	2 June	Bridlington Sailing Club	Withernsea	26.2	761.9
35	3 June	Withernsea	Chapel St Leonard	37.2	799.1
36	4 June	Chapel St Leonard	Wells-Next-The-Sea	31.3	830.4
37	5 June	Wells-Next-The-Sea	Happisburgh	36	866.4
38	6 June	REST DAY	REST DAY	0	866.4
39	7 June	REST DAY	REST DAY	0	866.4
40	8 June	REST DAY	REST DAY	0	866.4
41	9 June	Happisburgh	Aldeburgh	51.7	918.1
42	10 June	Aldeburgh	Orford Haven	11.6	929.7
43	11 June	REST DAY	REST DAY	0	929.7
44	12 June	Orford Haven	Joss Bay	47.8	977.5
45	13 June	Joss Bay	St Margaret's Bay	16.6	994.1

Day	Date	Start	End	Miles	Total Miles
46	14 June	St Margaret's Bay	Hastings	45.4	1039.5
47	15 June	Hastings	Cuckmere Haven	20.3	1059.8
48	16 June	Cuckmere Haven	Cuckmere Haven	3.75	1063.6
49	17 June	Cuckmere Haven	Littlehampton	32.9	1096.5
50	18 June	Littlehampton	Thornes Bay	40.7	1137.2
51	19 June	Thornes Bay	Swanage	30.1	1167.3
52	20 June	Swanage	Portland Harbour	24.7	1192
53	21 June	Portland Harbour	Seaton	36.3	1228.3
54	22 June	Seaton	Budleigh Salterton	15.7	1244
55	23 June	REST DAY	REST DAY	0	1244
56	24 June	Budleigh Salterton	Brixham	22.8	1266.8
57	25 June	Brixham	Dartmouth	10.9	1277.7
58	26 June	Dartmouth	Wembury	32.8	1310.5
59	27 June	Wembury	Pentewan	31.7	1342.2
60	28 June	Pentewan	Kennack Sands	31.2	1373.4
61	29 June	REST DAY	REST DAY	0	1373.4
62	30 June	REST DAY	REST DAY	0	1373.4
63	1 July	Kennack Sands	Mousehole	22	1395.4
64	2 July	Mousehole	St Ives	30.3	1425.7
65	3 July	St Ives	Trevose Head	34.2	1459.9
66	4 July	Trevose Head	Bude	29	1488.9
67	5 July	Bude	Lundy Island	24.4	1513.3
68	6 July	Lundy Island	Caldey Island	38.6	1551.9
69	7 July	Caldey Island	Angle Bay	23.5	1575.4
70	8 July	Angle Bay	Fishguard	38.8	1614.2
71	9 July	Fishguard	Llangranog	24.7	1638.9
72	10 July	REST DAY	REST DAY	0	1638.9

Day	Date	Start	End	Miles	Total Miles
73	11 July	Llangranog	Porth Oer	51.8	1690.7
74	12 July	Porth Oer	Dinas Dinlle	24.4	1715.1
75	13 July	Dinas Dinlle	Llaneilian	38.1	1753.2
76	14 July	REST DAY	REST DAY	0	1753.2
77	15 July	REST DAY	REST DAY	0	1753.2
78	16 July	Llaneilian	Douglas	55.6	1808.8
79	17 July	Douglas	Bride	23.1	1831.9
80	18 July	Bride	Donaghadee	49.9	1881.8
81	19 July	Donaghadee	Glenarm	28.8	1910.6
82	20 July	Glenarm	Machrihanish	39.6	1950.2
83	21 July	REST DAY	REST DAY	0	1950.2
84	22 July	Machrihanish	Island of Danna	36.6	1986.8
85	23 July	Island of Danna	Lochaline	45.9	2032.7
86	24 July	Lochaline	Strontian	31.3	**2064**

Appendix III
The Beaufort Scale

Scale	Kind of Wind	Wind Speed		Effects of Wind	
		MPH	Km/h	Earth	Sea
F0	Calm	<1	<1	Smoke rises vertically	Flat sea
F1	Very Light	1-3	1-5	Smoke drifts in direction of wind	Small ripples without crests
F2	Light Breeze	4-7	6-11	Wind can be felt on face	Small wavelets with unbroken crests.
F3	Gentle Breeze	8-12	12-19	Leaves on trees shake	Large wavelets; crests begin to break; scattered whitecaps
F4	Moderate Breeze	13-17	20-28	Dust and loose papers lifted	Small waves with breaking crests; frequent whitecaps
F5	Fresh Breeze	18-24	29-38	Small branches on trees shake	Moderate waves of some length; many whitecaps; small amounts of spray
F6	Strong Breeze	25-30	39-49	Big branches shake	Bigger wave; white foam crests very frequent; some airborne spray
F7	Near Gale	31-38	50-61	Impedes walking	The sea swells up; white foam forms when waves break up; moderate amounts of airborne spray

Scale	Kind of Wind	Wind Speed		Effects of Wind	
		MPH	Km/h	Earth	Sea
F8	Gale	39-46	62-74	Big trees shake	Moderately high waves with breaking crests; well-marked streaks blown in direction of wind.
F9	Strong Gale	47-54	75-88	Chimney pots and slates removed	High waves, dense foam blown in the direction of the wind; large amounts of airborne spray may reduce visibility
F10	Storm	55-63	89-102	Trees uprooted	Very high waves with overhanging crests; the sea looks completely white; waves fall down violently
F11	Violent Storm	64-72	103-117	Serious devastation	Exceptionally high waves; very large patches of foam cover much of sea surface; spray severely reduces visibility.
F12	Hurricane	>72	>117	Very serious catastrophes	Huge waves; sea is completely white because of foam and spray; air filled with driving spray greatly reducing visibility

Appendix IV

Glossary

Bivvy - Short for 'bivouac', meaning to camp without the use of a tent.

Breaking wave - When the wave becomes so steep that the crest begins to tumble down the face.

Clapotis - When two wave patterns are moving in near opposite directions (often as they are reflected from a cliff-face, rocks or breakwater) they may combine to form particularly big waves with tall, pyramidal crests and steep sides. They are difficult to predict and can be extremely violent. Such conditions are described as clapotis.

Fetch – The distance travelled by wind or waves across open water. Generally, the bigger the fetch, the bigger the waves.

F3, F4, F5 etc. - This refers to the strength of the wind as described in the Beaufort Scale. This scale is based on observation rather than an accurate measurement. Developed in 1805 by Francis Beaufort, an officer of the Royal Navy, this is the most widely used system to measure the wind today and is always used in shipping forecasts. A full explanation of this scale can be found in Appendix II.

Gunwale (pronounced gunnel) - The upper edge of the canoe's hull.

Hull - The main body of the canoe including the bottom and sides.

Leeboard - A pivoting keel attached to the side of the canoe.

Mizzen - A sail which is aft (to the rear) of, and is smaller than, the main sail. We sometimes dropped our larger sail and moved our small sail to the main sail position. At this point, this smaller sail is no longer a mizzen and becomes the main sail.

Neap tides – Every fortnight, around the time of a 'half-moon' the gravitational pull of the moon is at right angles to the gravitational pull of the sun. This causes a more even distribution of water on the earth's surface so that the tides, tidal streams and tidal range are less pronounced. At times when the moon is further away from the earth, the tides are small, and do not go out or come in as far as usual. At certain times of the year the moon is further from the earth and is said to be "in apogee". Therefore, the associated tides are appropriately small.

Overfall - Where a fast-flowing tidal stream meets a shoaling sea-bed, then upward-moving water currents can occur to create a disturbed water surface. Such disturbance can manifest itself as an oily-looking "boil" of water, or can cause irregular, unpredictable, steep-sided, pyramidal waves. They have crests that may be bursting upwards and in extreme cases the scale and violence can be extreme. Overfalls often form in conjunction with tide races.

RIB (Rigid Inflatable Boat) – A lightweight but high-performance boat, constructed with a rigid hull bottom which is joined to side-forming air tubes that are inflated to a high pressure so as to give resilient rigidity to the boat's sides.

Riffle – An area where the water flow is broken causing a disturbed water surface, similar to a mini rapid.

Spring tide - Once a fortnight, the gravitational pull of the moon comes into line with the gravitational pull of the sun. This occurs close to the "new" moon and "full" moon. It causes a larger than usual bulge of water to form. Consequently, both the tides and the tidal streams are more pronounced at this time, producing a greater "tidal range". This means that the tide comes in further and goes out further than usual. Since greater volumes of water are being moved about, the tidal streams are also swifter. At certain times of the year the moon is closer to the earth than at others. At these times the moon is said to be "in perigee"; it will be exerting a stronger gravitational pull and therefore producing exceptionally big spring tides.

Surf - An area of breaking waves, usually close to the shoreline but also over reefs and shoals.

Swell - Waves may continue to travel long distances from the point on the earth's surface where they are first generated and they become more regular in form as they do so. Such waves are known as the swell.

Tidal range - The difference in the height of the sea between low tide and high tide.

Tidal set - The direction towards which the tidal stream is moving.

Tidal stream - The horizontal movement of the sea as large bodies of water are moved in response to the same forces that cause the vertical movement (see below).

Tide - The vertical movement of the sea in relation to the shoreline or the sea bed, caused by the gravitational pull of the sun and moon.

Tide races and overfalls - Tide races and overfalls often occur in conjunction with one another. As such, throughout this book, I have often used the term "tide race" or "race" to describe both.

Tide race (tidal rapid) - Where a fast-flowing tidal stream is constricted – as off a headland or between islands – the constriction causes acceleration and the associated water movements can be exceptionally violent. This is particularly so when the wind blows against the direction of flow, so that the increased friction between the water surface and the air moving over it causes particularly large waves.

Wave - Most waves encountered on the sea have been generated by the wind, where movements of air disturb the water surface because of friction. The result is ripple patterns of varying size, according to the forces generated and the disturbance and the distance over which the wind is travelling, more properly called the "fetch."

Wave crest - The highest part of the wave.

Wave trough - The lowest part of the wave.

Yard - A spar on a mast from which the sail is set.